RANCHERS RAMBLERS & RENEGADES

True Tales of Territorial New Mexico

by
Marc Simmons

Ancient City Press
Santa Fe, New Mexico

International Standard Book Number:
0-941270-17-3
Library of Congress Catalogue Number:
83-073398

Second Printing
First Edition

Designed by Mary Powell

Typesetting by Business Graphics, Inc.
Albuquerque, New Mexico
Printed in the United States of America
by Inter-Collegiate Press
Shawnee Mission, Kansas

Dedicated to my friends, the Oteros
George, Jacque, Kevin & Jeffrey

Contents

Preface

I can hardly remember a time when I was not engaged in tracking down fascinating bits and pieces of New Mexico History. People often ask: "But hasn't it all been done? Haven't the best and most interesting parts of the story been collected long ago and written about?" I can only shake my head in dismay. For history is never complete, and the historian who closes his writing with an indelible period, convinced that he has produced the last word on a subject, is both foolish and ignorant.

History is not everything that happened in the past; it is only that portion which was somehow recorded or that remains accessible in the reminiscences of a few old-timers. So digging up the past is an on-going process, a continuing search for new records and a constant re-examination of those that have long been known and used. I find it the most joyous of pursuits.

Ranchers, Ramblers and Renegades should be considered a companion volume to my *Taos to Tomé: True Tales of Hispanic New Mexico,* first published by Adobe Press in 1978 and now available through Ancient City Press. That too was a collection of historical vignettes, but one dealing mainly with the Spanish colonial period. This work focuses attention on the territorial years, and I have tried to illuminate some of the lesser known incidents and characters of New Mexican history during the latter half of the nineteenth century and the early part of the twentieth.

Although basically a scholar and author of academic monographs, I have long acknowledged, in company with a minority of my colleagues, that the writing of what is usually termed "popular history" serves an important function. Simply put, it introduces the lay reader to the pleasures and usefulness of historical study. Personally, I have no patience with those shortsighted and selfish academicians who erect walls of pedantry and professional jargon around their field in a bid to maintain exclusiveness and keep out the uninitiated.

The articles collected here have appeared previously in the *Santa Fe Reporter,* the *New Mexico Independent,* the *El Paso Times, Westport Historical Quarterly, La Gaceta,* and *New Mexico Magazine.* Most have been altered or expanded since their original publication. Since this book, like the original articles, is intended for a general audience and contains no bibliography or academic footnotes, a word regarding the sources I have used is in order.

In the course of my scholarly research into a multiplicity of subjects associated with New Mexico history, I often encounter brief stories or small nuggets of information that seem interesting enough to use as the basis for my regular weekly newspaper column or for a popular magazine article. That material, mostly drawn from old documents, early tabloids, original diaries and the like, is of a primary nature, that is, it was set down by contemporary observers who were on the scene. Thus it retains a strong sense of the past and conveys a feeling for the reality of an earlier time.

The account of young Jane Wilson's dolorous captivity among the Comanches in 1853, related below, provides an example. Details of the incident, which grabbed headlines all over the nation, were included in many publications of the day. I used a number of those in telling about her ordeal, but I relied principally on New Mexico governor David Meriwether's autobiography (he was personally involved in the case) and on statements by the Territorial attorney William W. H. Davis in his authoritative book, *El Gringo: or, New Mexico and Her People* (1857).

As a historian dedicated to the canons of truth, I have made every effort to be as factual as possible. Nevertheless, some portions of what follows may appear to stretch both the imagination and credulity beyond acceptable limits. I can only suggest to any disbelieving reader that he embark upon his own study of territorial New Mexico, and I can practically guarantee that his research will produce firm evidence of marvels quite as extraordinary as any to be met in the pages of this book.

Finally, I would like to acknowledge the help of my typist, Susie Henderson, and the assistance of Orlando Romero, Sherry Smith-Gonzáles, Liz Dear, Ted and Vivian Steinbock, Janet Lecompte, David Weber, John L. Kessell, and John Erickson. My gratitude also extends to Marta Weigle and Mary Powell of the Ancient City Press.

Cerrillos, New Mexico   Marc Simmons
September 1983

Introduction

New Mexico, for an assortment of historical reasons, stayed a territory longer than any other area of the United States. From 1850 when they were granted formal territorial status by Congress to 1912 when the blessings of statehood were finally achieved, the New Mexican people remained political stepchildren to the rest of the nation.

In politics could be found one of the major causes for that situation. Many Washington congressmen were long opposed to admitting New Mexico to the family of states while its population remained ill-educated and unable to speak English. They had the distinct impression, too—even as the nineteenth century drew to a close—that the sun-baked lands along the far Rio Grande still formed an untamed frontier where lawful behavior and civilized amenities were notable for their scarcity. That view had some basis in fact, for in New Mexico and neighboring Arizona Indian wars of the most appalling nature lasted longer than anywhere else in the country.

Territorial governor Miguel Antonio Otero called attention to another important reason in his memoirs. "New Mexico," he declared with authority, "was located so as to receive the backwash from two streams. From one side Texas, Kansas, Colorado, and the Indian Territory deposited their flotsam and jetsam of humanity, while from the other side Utah, Arizona, and California spewed their human refuse. New Mexico became a sort of catch basin for this type."

While it is true that many of the outlaws and rogues were new arrivals, it must be acknowledged that the Territory produced its full share of the home-grown variety. There may have been something in the dry, intoxicating air, an intangible ether, that entered the lungs and caused an infection of the spirit which made people contentious, short-tempered, and prone to violence.

Young John Greiner of Ohio arrived in Santa Fe in July 1851 to become the Indian agent for New Mexico. Within a few weeks he wrote home to a friend expressing wonderment that here, "everybody and everything appear to be at cross purposes. Even the missionaries are at loggerheads." It was a social condition, so Spanish documents reveal, that had existed since colonial times.

In territorial days men with a short fuse became as common as thorns on a cactus. They sparked and then fueled the bloody Lincoln and Colfax county wars. They kept territorial politics in turmoil. They stole land grants and jumped mining claims. And they assailed their enemies with fiery words in the press or on occasion provoked gunfights and shot down their foes in the streets.

It was just this state of affairs which led General William T. Sherman in the 1860s to proclaim, with more seriousness than humor, that the Territory was so troublesome and worthless the United States ought to force Mexico to take it back. Equally perturbed, Governor Lew Wallace a decade later uttered his much-quoted, barbed observation: "Every calculation based on experience elsewhere fails in New Mexico."

Unfortunately, outlawry and political double-dealing were merely added to the poverty, hardship and general misery on the list of woes that seemingly had always afflicted the New Mexican populace. A Spanish friar of the seventeenth century once described New Mexico as "this miserable Kingdom," a descriptive phrase deriving from his unhappy encounter with the harsh winter climate, land that grudgingly yielded a subsistence and people who had grown accustomed to hunger, lice and unending isolation. Thereafter it is astonishing to observe the frequency with which the words "misery" and "miserable" pepper official government reports and correspondence dealing with domestic life in New Mexico.

Nor did wretched discomfort and unhappiness disappear overnight with the American conquest in 1846 and bestowal of the blessings of Yankeedom. For decades life remained dangerous, uncertain, and austere. Famines and epidemics persisted as in times past. For many rural New Mexicans, the words "hope" and "progress" existed outside their vocabularies.

Yet the prolonged territorial period was actually an era of transition, a time filled with events heralding a new stability in a more prosperous day. Furthermore, not all was unrelieved misery and tribulation. Even on the worst of occasions Hispanos and newly arrived Anglos found solace in social gatherings, sports, games and practical jokes. The small glimmers of humor that crept into the pages of our territorial history remind us of the resiliency of the human spirit.

Some examples can be found in the records of General Stephen W. Kearny's Army of the West which seized and occupied New Mexico in 1846, at the outbreak of the Mexican War. After a grueling march across the plains, on which the soldiers had endured short rations, bouts of dysentery, swarms of mosquitos, sunburn and the death of one man from an infected tarantula bite, Santa Fe in all its dusty backwardness rose to view like the Promised Land beyond the River Jordan. Soon after their arrival the trail-weary troopers threw aside their cares and produced a series of plays and minstrel shows for their own and the town's amusement. Their presentation, described below, became the social event of the season.

Later in the year, part of the army pushed down the Rio Grande and on Christmas Day fought and won a battle with Mexican soldiers at Brazito near Mesilla. Unopposed, they continued on to El Paso (then within the jurisdiction of New Mexico) where the entire population turned out to watch the American advance. Private John Hughes, keeping a diary, described people standing on rooftops, barns, and every other elevation that offered a view.

One of Kearny's soldiers suggested firing a salute with the cannon to provide a show for the throng. At once powder was poured down the throat of one of the cannon captured at Brazito, but nothing could be found to use as a blank shot. In the emergency a trooper sat down, pulled off his sweaty socks, rolled them into a ball and rammed it down on top of the powder.

"In the hurry," writes Hughes, "no attention was paid to the direction of the gun. When it was fired the socks hit a soldier in the face. Though not injured, he raised a great cry. He complained that he'd rather have been hit with a real cannon ball than a pair of socks worn from Fort Leavenworth to El Paso, without change for eight months. He demanded the gunners be punished."

Unlike the well-educated Hughes, who was a former Missouri school teacher, most of the men in this army were rustic country bumpkins, just off the farm. Spanish was utterly foreign to them and its proper pronunciation beyond their ability. In New Mexico platefuls of frijoles were added to the army mess. But since no one could say the word, *frijoles* was mangled to become "freeholders."

Dr. Adolph Wislizenus, a German doctor accompanying the troops, fared scarcely better than the lowly bean. To the men, his name sounded like "Whistling Jesus," and that's what he was called throughout the campaign.

During the succeeding territorial years, humor continued to serve the cowboy, farmer, miner, sheepherder and railroad laborer as a palliative, alleviating some of the stress and physical hardship associated with daily life and work. A true incident that happened in the ranch country on the eastern plains illustrates the point.

It concerns a top cowhand, August Johnson. While he was tending cattle on July 3, 1882, a thunderstorm came up and lightning struck and killed him. Cowboys who had known him were in the habit of remarking thereafter: "The third of July in '82 was the last of August!"

New Mexico's territorial period offers a fertile field for human interest stories. Ages of turmoil, conflict and swift change may be exceedingly hard on the people who experience them, but they provide authors with bountiful material and readers with abundant opportunity to gain new insights about the human condition. In that lies both the joy and the value in any study of history.

A Priest Who Did His Duty

Under a marble slab in the San José Cemetery on the outskirts of Juarez lie the remains of a man who left an indelible mark on the history of New Mexico. He was Ramón Ortiz, priest and humanitarian, who was born in Santa Fe in 1813.

From the days of earliest settlement on the upper Rio Grande, the Ortiz's distinguished themselves as soldiers and civil officers in the service of the king. Ramón's own father, who died just before he was born, had been the *alferez real,* or royal sheriff, of the city of Santa Fe. His mother, Doña Teresa, died a few months after giving birth. Before she died, she made her eldest daughter promise that the infant Ramón would be raised for the priesthood.

Ramón's sister and foster mother, Ana María, married Colonel Antonio Vizcarra. A noted Indian fighter, he defeated the hostile Navajo in western New Mexico and served for a brief time as the provincial governor. The Colonel became Ramón's idol, and the boy began to think that a career in the military rather than the church was what he wanted. However, because of the pledge to his mother, when Ramón was nine the family packed him off to a seminary in Durango, Mexico.

Over the next few years he worked hard at his studies, all the while restless and miserable. In plaintive letters to Colonel Vizcarra he begged for permission to leave the school and take up the life of a soldier. Finally the Colonel became so worried about his foster son that he made a journey south to Durango. There, after long discussion the two agreed that Ramón should abandon plans for the priesthood and instead go to France and enter a military academy.

Ramón's joy was short-lived. A cholera epidemic broke out in Durango a few days later, and Colonel Vizcarra was one of the first to die. When they heard the news Ana María and her sisters wrote from Santa Fe expressing the belief that the Colonel's death was divine vengeance bought on by Ramón's decision to defy his dead mother's last wish. In despair the boy remained at the seminary and was soon ordained a priest.

For the next five years he served as a missionary in a small Indian village in northern Mexico. Then he was assigned to administer the church of Guadalupe at El Paso del Norte (modern Juarez). There he would remain for the next half century, becoming a key figure in the turbulent events that swirled across the Southwest.

The name of Father Ramón Ortiz first gained wide currency, in the

Church and plaza at El Paso. (From John Russell Bartlett, *Personal Narrative of Explorations and Incidents in Texas, New Mexico, California, and Chihuahua,* 1856.)

United States at least, during the aftermath of the ill-fated Texan-Santa Fe expedition. The president of the Republic of Texas, M. B. Lamar, had sent a force of several hundred men to New Mexico in 1841. Its purpose, so he claimed, was to open peaceful trade. But New Mexico's governor, Manuel Armijo, chose to regard the movement as an armed invasion. He arrested the entire party and started them on the road south under an escort headed by Captain Damacio Salazar.

Salazar's treatment of the prisoners in the desert between Socorro and El Paso was nothing less than barbaric. Those who fell ill or could not keep up were killed. Others were beaten and robbed of their few personal possessions.

When the survivors straggled into El Paso the military commandant General J. Elias y González was appalled at their condition. At once he suspended Captain Salazar and sent him back to Santa Fe in disgrace. Then he summoned Father Ortiz and asked him to feed and clothe the starving and ragged Texans.

At this time the padre had a large home presided over by his several sisters who had recently joined him and staffed with many servants. With arrival of the prisoners the house became a bustle of activity. The women set about sewing shirts and underclothing. Servants hauled water from the irrigation ditches for baths. Piles of food appeared magically on the tables. Ortiz appealed to his friends for donations of shoes, medicines, bandages and shaving instruments. Under the priest's guidance the town opened its heart to the suffering men.

Among the Texans was George W. Kendall, a young journalist from New Orleans. It was he who published a popular book on the episode several years later and recounted the unstinting charity of Padre Ortiz and his flock. When it was time to continue the journey toward Chihuahua the father loaned his own carriage to Kendall and others so they would not have to walk. Later the newspaperman wrote with gratitude, "Seldom have I parted from a friend with more real regret than with Ortiz, and as I shook him by the hand for the last time, and bade him perhaps an eternal adieu, I thought if ever a noble heart beat in man it was in the breast of this young generous priest."

Again at the time of the Mexican War Americans had occasion to benefit from the padre's kindness. Late in 1846, Colonel Alexander Doniphan marched down the Rio Grande and seized El Paso. One of his first acts was to arrest Father Ortiz who, as an intense patriot, had been sending messengers to Chihuahua with information on the enemy advance.

As Doniphan started down the road toward the capture of Chihuahua City he took the priest along as a prisoner. Ortiz was allowed to travel in his own coach which he had stocked with ample food and water. In the midst of the desert the army's provisions gave out. The good father voluntarily distributed his own provisions to the hungry and thirsty soldiers. His first thought was always for others, friend or foe.

When the war ended Ortiz went to Mexico City and tried unsuccessfully to block ratification of the treaty of Guadalupe-Hidalgo which delivered his beloved New Mexico into American hands. Afterward he rode up and down the Rio Grande trying to persuade New Mexicans to abandon their homes and move across the new border. About three thousand responded and migrated into northern Mexico.

From his residence in Juarez Father Ortiz continued to exercise influence on both sides of the international boundary. Whenever problems arose he was always one of the first to be called in as a mediator. His reputation as a friend of the poor, ready to help anyone in need, became legendary. He raised dozens of orphans in his home and more than once took the blanket off his own bed and gave it to a penniless beggar.

When, old and blind, he died from cancer in 1896, the *El Paso Times* expressed the sentiment of residents on both sides of the border when it wrote: "His good heart was full of kindness, his nature was gentleness itself, and he did good for the love of doing it. No wonder the good people loved their priest almost to adoration."

Cock Fighting— New Mexico Style

Few people are aware that the bloody sports of bull fighting and cock fighting were popular in New Mexico a century ago. To celebrate Mexico's independence from Spain in 1821 the citizens of Santa Fe built a temporary bullring on the main plaza and held fights as part of the general festivities of the hour. A few other bull fights are recorded during the next twenty-five years. Then in 1846, with the annexation of the territory by the United States, the new officials put a stop to such things.

Cock fighting, however, lingered on almost to the end of the century. It survived particularly in remote rural villages, far from the disapproving eyes of the government. Many a man was enriched and many another became impoverished during the excitement and wild betting that accompanied a good fight. Entire towns would turn out to cheer on their favorite game cock and make wagers against a rival town.

In the midst of a heated encounter, when it appeared that one bird or the other was gaining an advantage, bets would be doubled or tripled by shouting spectators. If a rooster went down long odds might be given against him, but they were nearly always accepted. The unexpected had a way of intervening; it was not uncommon for a nearly spent contestant to get in a lucky punch and finish his opponent. That led to a common native saying, "A fight is won at the finish, not at the start."

Given the large sums of money that changed hands at a fight it is not surprising that the raising and preparation of game cocks was a serious business among early day New Mexicans. Young birds were kept in isolation and semi-darkness, tied by one leg with a piece of string to a stake. Periodically the owner and a helper brought in another rooster, raised in similar confinement, to rehearse them in the art of fighting. With each man holding a bird in his hands, thrusts were made to arouse their anger to fever pitch. Come the day of a fight, they were primed for battle.

Some game cocks were placed under the care and supervision of specialized trainers. A good trainer became so familiar with the qualities of his rooster that his handling and encouragement during the fight might well spell the difference between winning and losing.

Another professional associated with the business was the *amarrador,* the man who tied the small razor-sharp blades on the feet of the birds. The proper attachment of these blades was considered an art because if they were lost in the course of the fight the rules forbade their being replaced.

Cock fights were always held in the open. The "pit" was merely a circle drawn on the ground with a sharp stick. The audience formed an outer ring, men kneeling in front and others standing behind. On signal the trainers released their entries and the struggle began. The blades on the feet and the sharp beaks insured that feathers would fly and blood would splash. Usually the same cocks fought to the death, and it was not uncommon for both birds to be killed.

Cock fighting was not confined to the Hispano communities. Many Anglos in the new mining camps took up the sport with enthusiasm. For a time the most famous game cock in New Mexico was owned by Squire Hartt of Taos.

With the opening of the twentieth century many citizens decided that cock fighting was giving the territory an unsavory reputation. In 1900 the legislature passed a law strictly prohibiting the practice. Overnight game cocks disappeared and the story of cock fighting became a part of history.

Amateur Theatrics

The first play in the Southwest was written and produced during the early summer of 1598 by Captain Farfán de los Godos. He was one of colonizer Juan de Oñate's officers, and his little drama, staged under cottonwoods in the El Paso Valley, celebrated the Spaniards' safe arrival at the doorway to New Mexico.

Soon after the Oñate expedition reached San Juan Pueblo on the upper Rio Grande, its members organized another theatrical presentation. This one was a traditional folk drama brought from Spain: *Los Moros y los Cristianos*. Enacted outdoors and on horseback, it is still performed in New Mexico today.

A variety of other Hispanic folk plays were presented throughout the colonial period—whenever people got together for a religious holiday or fiesta. Americans entering the region after independence in 1821 were amazed to see the crowds these events attracted.

After General Stephen W. Kearny conquered New Mexico in 1846, some of the soldiers in his army of occupation decided to try their hand at dramatic productions. Their effort, launched at Santa Fe that same year, represented the first English-language theater in the Southwest. Amateurish though it was, it proved a booming success.

The group of troopers formed a "Thespian Association." Membership came mainly from the Laclede Rangers, a company of Missouri Volunteers who had enlisted in St. Louis. Governor Charles Bent gave them permission to use a room in the historic Governors Palace for their theater.

Sets were designed and painted. Musicians were found in the army and an orchestra was organized. Costumes were arranged for. Dresses, needed by the men playing female parts, were borrowed from distinguished Spanish ladies in Santa Fe. The rehearsals hummed.

The moving spirit behind all the feverish activity was Private Bernard McSorley. He served both as stage manager and star actor.

The play in preparation was *Pizarro, or the Death of Rolla*, originally written in German in 1796 and introduced to British and American audiences in English translation by the end of the century. It was a romantic tragedy, widely popular among theater-goers.

Private McSorley took the role of Pizarro and two other Rangers impersonated female actors. According to advance billing the part of Elvira was played by *Miss* Edward Shands, and Cora by *Miss* William

Jameson. Afterward it was reported that, "the *female* performers did their best to look the characters, as well as act them." The town's uppercrust ladies who attended did not understand the English dialogue, but they enjoyed the orchestra and were amused at the impersonation of women by soldiers in disguise.

The play was followed on the same bill by a minstrel show under the direction of John T. Neal, also a private in the Rangers. It was composed of "songs interspersed with Negro lectures, conundrums, etc., all in the style of broad extravaganza. Each was received with thunders of applause."

To understand one bit of the minstrel's humor we must know that since arrival in New Mexico the common soldier had been fed a steady diet of bread made from unsifted flour, all that was available locally. In the show one black-face actor asked another, "Why are the Missouri Volunteers like ladies' bustles?" The answer was, "Because they are both stuffed with bran." That brought down the house. Soldiers the world over have laughed at jokes that make fun of their hard lot.

In his diary one of the American troopers wrote: "Last night the theater went off well and was attended by such a large crowd that there was great inconvenience on this account. The priest was present, as well as many of the best women, all of whom enjoyed it and were much pleased."

Indeed, the affair was such a hit that the Laclede Rangers offered another stirring bill the following month. A printed poster circulated around Santa Fe listed two plays to appear on the same program—*Barbarossa!* and the farce *Fortune's Frolic.* The evening was to conclude with the Virginia Minstrels singing "Spanish Gals," "Blue Tail Fly," and the ever popular "You Ain't Good-Looking and You Can't Come In."

Thus it was that General Kearny's rough soldiers launched New Mexico's theater in English. In later years professional plays with real actors became commonplace, but none were offered with as much enthusiasm as those first given by the Laclede Rangers.

Headquarters building, Fort Marcy, Santa Fe, ca. 1880. Photograph by Fred Muller. (Neg. no. 1732, courtesy Museum of New Mexico.)

Captain Jack Crawford, the ''Poet Scout.'' Photograph by Ben Wittick. (Neg. no. 102037, courtesy Museum of New Mexico.)

The Poet Scout

Scattered throughout the West in the early part of this century were many old-timers who delighted in recounting their adventures on the frontier. Some of them found that with a little showmanship they could turn their past experiences into a fast buck. Buffalo Bill and Pawnee Bill, suitably bewhiskered and clad in fringed buckskins, set the style. With considerable theatrical promotion they were able to capitalize on America's fascination with the Wild West.

One man who took a leaf from their notebook was New Mexico's own Captain Jack Crawford, nicknamed the "Poet Scout." Virtually forgotten today, Captain Jack's name was once a household word in the Territory.

Born of Scotch parents in Ireland in 1847, John Wallace (Jack) Crawford immigrated to America with his impoverished family when he was seven. It is said that he got off the boat wearing Scottish kilts. Put to work in a Pennsylvania coal mine, the lad had no chance for schooling.

When the Civil War broke out he tried to enlist at age fourteen. But the Governor of Pennsylvania is reported to have told him, "Go back to your mother, boy. We are organizing an army, not a Sunday school class!"

Somehow Jack managed, a few months later, to slip past the enlistment officer. Shortly afterward he was badly wounded at the Battle of Spottsylvania and sent to a hospital in Philadelphia. There a sympathetic nun taught him to read and write during his convalescence.

As a young man hungry for excitement, Jack Crawford went West. In the Sioux War of 1876 he served as a scout and messenger for Generals Wesley Merritt and George Crook. That same year he succeeded Buffalo Bill Cody as chief of scouts. When Apache troubles flared along the Mexican border, Captain Jack headed for the Southwest. Over the next decade his exploits against hostile Indians became legendary.

One incident of note occurred in 1880. Chief Victorio had been launching bloody raids on west Texas and New Mexico from his base in the mountains of Mexico. Colonel George Buell decided to send an army scout on "a very dangerous mission." He would search out the Apache chief and try to persuade him to surrender.

At first no scout would accept the assignment. Then Jack Crawford volunteered. Taking an Indian named Navajo Charlie as interpreter and another man named Casimero from Fort Craig, he headed south across the border. At every high point Captain Jack sent up smoke signals to let Victorio know he was coming. One night by the light of the moon and campfire he wrote a sentimental poem of three verses and three choruses, perhaps to take his mind off the risky job at hand.

One day he spotted the Apache camp with his spy glass, just a mile away. He ordered Navajo Charlie to go in and invite the chief out for a talk. The interpreter absolutely refused. In his official account Captain Jack said "Coaxing and threats alike failed to move him. In my anger I would have gone myself into the hostile camp, but I knew not enough of the Apache tongue to converse with Victorio, and he nor none of his warriors could speak English."

Reluctantly the Captain returned north toward El Paso, his mission a failure. But the episode added luster to his reputation, since he had braved dangerous country where no other scout would go. Later he won more laurels serving under General Nelson A. Miles in the Geronimo campaign.

Much of Crawford's career in New Mexico was centered at Fort Craig on the Rio Grande below Socorro. In addition to his occasional scouting duties he served as the postmaster and post trader. By 1882 he had opened the Scouts Hotel adjacent to the fort. He advertised it in Territorial newspapers as, "The soldier's home and bivouac, the miner's safe retreat."

A few years later he established a ranch at the nearby village of San Marcial. By that time Fort Craig had closed and he had been made care-taker of the abandoned buildings. He was assisted by his wife Maria, who had once cooked for the officers at the fort.

Captain Jack named his daughter May Cody Crawford in honor of his old friend Buffalo Bill. He also had a son, Harry, who worked as a cowboy in the San Andres Mountains and afterward became a conductor on the Santa Fe Railroad.

Business and theatrical ventures increasingly took the Poet Scout away from home. In his absence Maria was left to guard the fort. On more than one occasion she scared away midnight intruders with blasts from her shotgun.

Whenever Jack was preparing to depart, he would comb his flowing hair, don his beaded buckskins, and present himself to his wife for inspection. Upon being asked how he looked, she would always reply: "Silly!"

But others thought he cut quite a romantic figure and were willing to invest in his many business deals. For a while he owned a livery and sale stable at Chloride where his brother, Austin Crawford, was involved in mining. Captain Jack had long been interested in mines too.

As early as 1880 he had gone to Denver and convinced investors to put up ten million dollars for the purpose of "thoroughly prospecting and developing southern New Mexico." The *Santa Fe New Mexican* referred to his plans as "a huge scheme," but noted shortly that Crawford and his companions had discovered at least one good mine in the Black Range.

All this time Captain Jack was churning out not only poems but novels and plays as well. Some people had come to refer to him as the "Bobbie Burns of the West," but one sober critic said of his verses that "by no stretch of courtesy could they be called poetry."

In 1883 Crawford wrote a frontier drama which was presented at a historical celebration in Santa Fe. He played the starring role of an army scout. While in the capital he handed out what the press described as "cabinet-sized" photographs of himself with poetic inscriptions on the back.

As time passed, he was much in demand as a lecturer and reciter of his own verse. He did a stint in Buffalo Bill's Wild West Show and made a trip to England where he gave a command performance in the court of Queen Victoria. The Poet Scout was especially popular in New York where he made many appearances. He even established a second home in Brooklyn.

Along the way there were those who began to say that he was a phony and that tales of his bravery on the New Mexico frontier were much exaggerated. But an incident in 1893 put the scoffers in their place.

Captain Jack had gone to the Chicago fair accompanied by a band of befeathered Indians. The Studebaker Company had one of the most popular exhibits, which included the original coach of the Revolutionary War hero LaFayette. The building caught fire and it seemed the priceless coach would be lost, but New Mexico's Poet Scout and his Indians rushed into the flames and dragged it to safety.

The grateful Studebaker Company sent Crawford's daughter a pony cart and harness. She used it to ride between Fort Craig and San Marcial.

A short time before his death in Brooklyn in 1917, in a reflective mood, the aging scout told a reporter, "I am simply Jack Crawford, boy soldier, rustic poet, scout, and bad actor." He was also, we might add now, a picturesque character who deserves to be remembered.

Tricks Mirages Play

The thin, transparent air and unbroken distances characteristic of the Southwest are responsible for several optical phenomena which perplexed and astonished nineteenth-century travelers. One of the most common was the mirage, often encountered by riders on the Butterfield Trail west of El Paso and Mesilla and on the Santa Fe Trail in eastern New Mexico. Formerly called a "false pond," the mirage was an illusionary body of water that magically appeared on the distant horizon and then mysteriously vanished as one approached it. For a man with parched lips, eager for a drink, this deception of nature proved unnerving.

Santa Fe Trail wagonmaster Josiah Gregg described the effects of a mirage in his journal: "The thirsty wayfarer, after jogging for hours under a burning sky, at length spies a pond. Yes, it must be water! It looks too natural for him to be mistaken. He quickens his pace, but lo, as he approaches, it recedes and entirely disappears. And when on its apparent site, he finds but a parched plain under his feet."

Practically everyone who wrote on travel in the Southwest had something to say about the strange tricks of mirages. Most authors tried to come up with some kind of explanation. One theory held that the mirage resulted from the refraction of the sun's rays on the bare prairie or desert. But Gregg had a slightly different idea. He believed that false ponds came from "the reflection of light upon a gas emanating from the sun-scorched earth and vegetation."

Motorists in New Mexico today frequently see mirages on the highway. Stretches of road reaching toward the horizon appear to glisten with moisture as if a sudden rain had spread a narrow lake across the pavement.

The pioneers were also fooled by other natural distortions in the air. In the shimmering heat of a summer's day a herd of buffalo thirty miles away was greatly magnified and seemed to float in the sky. Tufts of grass or weeds on the distant horizon were often mistaken for Indians, causing wagon trains to circle up in a defensive position. And flocks of ravens hopping about on the prairie might be perceived as a herd of antelope.

The extraordinarily clear atmosphere tended to telescope space and make distant objects appear closer than they really were. Men who were accustomed to judging distance by eye in the humid East found that their calculations went considerably awry when they applied their usual standards of measurement in the Southwest.

Experiences of greenhorns in misjudging mileage provided plenty of amusement for old-timers. One stock tale, repeated endlessly around campfires, told of a beardless youth who climbed off a stagecoach his first day in New Mexico and surveyed the exhilarating landscape. Seeing a mountain which looked to be a quarter of a mile away he decided to undertake a short hike to its summit before lunch.

Hours later he returned, exclaiming that after walking for hours the mountain seemed no nearer than when he started. Bystanders lounging about the stage stop had a good laugh at his expense, and the young man was much embarrassed. He made a mental note that he would not be fooled again.

Afterward, on a stroll he came to an ankle-deep irrigation ditch that he wished to cross. A cowboy rode up, found the newcomer taking off his clothes and asked what he was doing.

"If it's as far across this body of water as it was to that mountain," answered the newcomer, "I'm preparing for a long swim."

An Early Glimpse
of the Mesilla Valley

A recently discovered diary of Mamie Bernard Aguirre, found in the trunk of one of her descendants, provides an intriguing look at life in the Mesilla Valley during the year 1864. Mamie was the daughter of Joab Bernard, a prominent storekeeper of Westport, Missouri (now part of Kansas City).

In his business Mr. Bernard catered to traders who came over the Santa Fe Trail from New Mexico. One of his customers was a handsome young merchant from Las Cruces named Don Epifanio Aguirre. Mamie became enamored of the dashing New Mexican and in August 1862, they were married in what has been described as the most lavish wedding ever to take place in Westport.

For a year the couple remained in the East, but in the fall of 1863 they started over the trail for Santa Fe. Mamie rode in an ambulance provided by her adoring husband. She had a new baby, Pedro, and a thirteen-year-old nurse named Angelina to help with diapers and such. The Aguirre caravan consisted of ten wagons, each drawn by ten mules and loaded with ten thousand pounds of freight.

Arriving in Santa Fe Don Epifanio delivered his goods and then continued on to his home downriver. Mamie notes in her diary, "We reached our long journey's end, Las Cruces, just a week before Christmas, having been over three months on the road."

The sights and sounds of the Mesilla Valley proved enchanting to an impressionable young woman straight from the East, for, as Mamie said, "There was something new to see all the time." One surprise came at the Christmas dinner shared with Epifanio's parents and grandparents. Dessert was a fresh watermelon cut late the previous season and hung near the rafters of the storeroom to preserve it.

Bunches of grapes were also served. "They raise huge quantities of grapes in the valley from which the celebrated El Paso wine is made. They are so sweet and keep very nicely til late in the winter packed in chopped straw."

Mamie was quite overwhelmed by the ceremony attached to the christening of her little son Pedro. "He being the first grandson in the family," she remarked, "a special celebration was made. For three days

Plaza at La Mesilla, oil on masonite. (Neg. no. 37917, courtesy Museum of New Mexico.)

before, there was a baker and two assistants in the house. They baked no end of cakes, and roasted fowls and pigs. Everything was cooked in one of those bee hive shaped adobe ovens that opened into the kitchen. The number of eggs that were used was a marvel."

Two hundred guests showed up for the christening, many coming by carriage from as far away as El Paso. The baby was toasted endlessly with champagne, and the huge feast was followed by an all-night dance. Breathless, Mamie wrote that "it was all a wonder to me!"

Greater excitement was in store the following March when she attended a bullfight in La Mesilla. A ring made of logs tied together with rawhide had been placed in the plaza facing the church. Private boxes, called *palcos*, were raised high on stilts for the viewing pleasure of the uppercrust like the Aguirres.

Mamie from Missouri got quite flustered when asked to climb a rickety ladder to the box. Her legs, and perhaps much else, would be exposed to the crowd below. But that problem was solved by two servants who rushed forward and shielded her with a blanket as she made the ascent.

"We all enjoyed the bullfight immensely," she recorded, "though there were no bulls killed and no blood shed."

Over the next six years Mamie, now with three sons, accompanied her husband on several trips back to Westport. But Las Cruces was home for her now, and she was always eager to return.

Then, in 1870, Don Epifanio made a business trip to Arizona. On the way his stagecoach was attacked by Apaches and he was killed. Heartsick, Mamie gathered up her children and went East to her father's home, carrying memories of joyous days in the Mesilla Valley.

A Matter of Words

In the latter part of the last century Don Felipe Chávez was the most prominent man in Belén a town on the Rio Grande between Albuquerque and Socorro. He owned an adobe mansion and a large store, both located on Main Street. His business interests were vast. He had investments in silver mines in Chihuahua and a broker in New York to care for his stock transactions.

At the time of his death in 1905, Don Felipe was regarded as one of the richest men in New Mexico. Indeed, he was commonly known by the nickname, "*El Millonario*." Legend has it that twice a year he hauled his horde of gold and silver coins onto the patio of his house. There he gave them a good airing, as he said, to prevent rust.

Felipe Chávez laid the foundation for his fortune at an early day when he joined his older brothers in the Santa Fe trade. They operated their own mule trains to Missouri where they purchased goods for resale in New Mexico.

One of his uncles, Antonio José Chávez, was held up by outlaws and murdered in 1843 on the Santa Fe Trail. The tragic event occurred in central Kansas on what became known as Chávez (now corrupted to Jarvis) Creek. Army troops captured the culprits and several were later hung. Part of the gold Antonio José had been carrying was recovered and returned to his heirs.

The Chávez family was well-known to the principal merchants of St. Louis and Kansas City. As a result Don Felipe enjoyed unlimited credit. Whenever he needed a load of goods, he put together a caravan of wagons and sent it East in charge of a trusted foreman. With him he sent a list of what was wanted: sugar, coffee, clothes, bolts of cloth, cosmetics, jewelry, candles, and the like.

One of the commercial houses Don Felipe dealt with in St. Louis was owned by Edward Glasgow. When Mr. Glasgow received an order from his old customer in New Mexico, he promptly supplied the articles requested and at the end of the year sent a bill for the total.

On a certain occasion he received the list from Chávez's wagon foreman and discovered that one of the items wanted was *un caso grande*. That was a large kettle of the kind commonly used in New Mexico to cook up chile stew for working men at lambing or shearing time. Now Mr. Glasgow knew Spanish very well, but he took that item to read *una casa grande*, a big house. Since he never failed to fill an order, he

25

promptly went out and purchased a nice St. Louis house in the name of Don Felipe Chávez of Belén, New Mexico.

When his caravan reached home Don Felipe went through the goods and discovered that for once his merchant friend had let him down. There was no kettle for the coming lambing season.

He promptly forgot the matter and did not think of it again until the end of the year when his annual bill arrived from St. Louis. Upon it he was astounded to discover the charge of $15,000 for "a big house."

A few months later Don Felipe had to go East on business. In St. Louis he went straight to Mr. Glasgow and announced that there was a mistake in his bill since he had never ordered a big house. They hunted up the original list, found how the error had been made and had a good laugh.

Felipe Chávez paid for the house and years afterward Glasgow sold it for him—at a price of $80,000. In telling of the incident later Don Felipe always said, with a twinkle in his eye, "What was a bad mistake worked out in the end." With luck like that, it is no wonder that he became "El Millonario."

Arrival of the caravan at Santa Fé. (From Josiah Gregg, *Commerce of the Prairies,* 1844.)

Tragedy on the Plains

The horrors of Indian captivity was a popular literary theme a century ago. Women and children, snatched from a log cabin in the eastern woods or carried off from a wagon train on the western plains, always had a thrilling and terrible story to tell if later they managed to escape or were ransomed. The subject held a grim fascination for the reading public, and publishers were quick to recognize it. How many captive tales were printed is difficult to say, but even a casual count suggests there must have been hundreds.

One of the best known incidents in early day New Mexico involved the seizure of Mrs. J. M. White and her ten-year-old daughter by Jicarilla Apaches. Since neither survived their ordeal, what we know about the matter comes from secondary accounts.

James White, a Missouri merchant, started for Santa Fe in the fall of 1849, traveling as a member of a large freight caravan. He was accompanied by his young wife, their daughter and Mrs. White's black female servant.

In the vicinity of modern Clayton White decided that the Indian danger had been passed. Eager to reach Santa Fe, he took his family, five companions and a baggage wagon and hurried on ahead. Near Point of Rocks, east of modern Springer, the Jicarillas struck. All the men were cut down and killed at once. The baggage was torn open, some items stolen, and the rest scattered on the prairie. Mrs. White, her child and servant were carried away.

Hours later the main caravan came upon the grisly scene—the upturned and broken wagon, the bodies and smell of death. Since no women were found it was assumed they had been made prisoners. That fact was soon confirmed when a hunting party of Pueblo Indians rode by and reported seeing an American lady and her little child traveling with an Apache war party.

That was grave news. At once riders were sent forth: one to Santa Fe with a report to New Mexico's Superintendent of Indian Affairs, James S. Calhoun, and another to Taos, the closest place at which soldiers were stationed. Agent Calhoun acted swiftly, as he reported in a dispatch to Washington: "I have just secured the services of a trader, Encarnacion Garcia, who knows the Apaches well, their haunts and trails. This man is well known to respectable people here, as a daring, fearless, and discreet man. I promised to pay him $1000 if he succeeds in bring-ing in to me Mrs. White and her daughter. He goes out quietly but rapidly, as a trader, and if he finds the object of his search, will doubtless secure them."

In spite of strenuous efforts Garcia failed in his mission. He wan-dered south for six weeks, visiting Indian camps, and finally reached the San Antonio-El Paso road at the southern end of the Guadalupe Mountains. But he could learn nothing of the captives.

In the meanwhile the army had entered the picture. The second rider sent from the scene of the tragedy had reached Taos and there reported to Major William Grier of the First U.S. Dragoons. Delays fol-lowed as troops and supplies were assembled in anticipation of a long pursuit.

By the time Major Grier was ready to depart he had enlisted as guide the veteran mountain man, Antoine Leroux. Fifty miles out of Taos the soldiers came to Rayado Creek where Kit Carson had recently taken up ranching. The famed scout was at home and when he learned of Mrs. White's captivity he promptly agreed to join the party as a scout.

Together, Leroux and Carson led the uniformed men across the plains to Point of Rocks. By the time they reached the scene of the massacre almost two weeks had elapsed and the trail had grown cold. But they pushed ahead, nevertheless, following faint signs that would have been invisible to other men. The tracking continued for twelve days over what Kit would later describe as "the most difficult trail I ever followed." At last they came to the Indian camp, which the warriors had rejoined af-ter their raid.

Carson saw the Apaches first and yelled at his companions to charge. But Leroux and Major Grier hung back, expressing a wish to hold a par-ley with the enemy. It was a fatal decision, for it cost the troops their element of surprise. It also cost poor Mrs. White her life.

The Indians, recovering from their astonishment, fled in every direction. In the confusion Mrs. White ran toward her rescuers. But sev-eral arrows pierced her heart and she fell dead. Declared Kit Carson long afterward, "I am certain that if the Indians had been charged immediately, she would have been saved."

One of the young soldiers, James Bennett, wrote in his diary: "We encamped and buried the remains of Mrs. White. She was a fraile, delicate, and very beautiful woman but having undergone such treat-ment as she had suffered, nothing but a wreck remained. Her face, even after death, indicated a sorrow-stricken, heart-broken, and hopeless creature."

Several days later, as the troops were returning to Taos, they cap-tured an Apache woman near the Wagon Mound. She informed them that the black servant had been killed soon after capture because she could not keep up. And the daughter of Mrs. White had been traded to the Utes.

For several years repeated efforts were made to find the child. The

Jicarilla Apache camp, ca. 1935. Photograph by T. Harmon Parkhurst. (Neg. no. 22673, courtesy Museum of New Mexico.)

story attracted national attention in the press and Congress appropriated $1,500 to be used for a ransom. The War Department provided a military escort for Isaac Dunn, Mrs. White's brother, who came from his home in Virginia to lead the search for his small niece. But the girl was never found.

Isaac and his brother James wrote to the Secretary of War expressing the hope that she had died because, as they put it, that was a better fate than being reared by barbarous savages. They also expressed a bitter desire to see the "extermination of every last Indian on the plains of New Mexico."

The affair also left Kit Carson with a sad memory. In the Apache camp, not far from Mrs. White's warm corpse, he had found some of her possessions, plundered from the wagon. Among them was a dime novel of the kind then wildly popular in the East. Its pages related the exploits of Kit Carson and represented him as slaying Indians by the hundreds.

"I have often thought," Kit told friends, "that Mrs. White must have read it, and knowing that I lived nearby, must have prayed for my appearance in order that she might be saved. I did come, but I lacked the power to persuade those that were in command to follow my plan for her rescue. They would not listen to me and they failed."

In spite of his words, Carson always felt that he too had failed. Perhaps it was because the dime novel pictured him as a man who always succeeded.

The Ghosts at Robbers' Roost

The Four Corners, which New Mexico shares with Arizona, Utah, and Colorado, is well-known. A handsome monument marks the site and during good weather Navajo Indian souvenir and food vendors set up stalls to cash in on the stream of tourists.

At the other side of the state the "Three Corners" where New Mexico, Oklahoma, and Colorado meet is unvisited. Few photographers ever show up to snap the small, unimposing marker and there are no vendors hawking their wares. But here is a scenic and isolated world that is rich in history.

For many miles the Colorado-New Mexico boundary in this area is straddled by a high tableland capped with dark lava. The far eastern end of this elevation, called Black Mesa, juts—but just barely—into the corner of Oklahoma. At 4978 feet, the tiny piece of mesa is the highest point in that state.

Rising in New Mexico, the storied Cimarron River crosses into Oklahoma at the hamlet of Kenton, ten miles or so south of the "Three Corners." Black Mesa hems in the river valley on the north as do a series of buttes and smaller mesas on the south. The unspoiled land is seamed by arroyos and deep canyons, precisely the sort of place that would have appealed to outlaws back when the West was untamed. It should come as no surprise, then, to discover that the rough country below Black Mesa was once known as Robbers' Roost.

That phrase was made famous by the late Zane Grey, who used it as the title of one of his romantic western novels. But in the old days there was more than one Robbers' Roost. The best-known spot to go by that name was the secluded outlaw camp of Butch Cassidy, located in the badlands of east central Utah. There were also the Ladron, or Thieves, Mountains northwest of Socorro, New Mexico. They too were sometimes spoken of as Robbers' Roost.

The badman hangout under the shadow of Black Mesa, however, was probably the original Roost. It lay in a two-mile-wide "neutral strip" that a survey error had left outside the jurisdiction of both New Mexico and Oklahoma. It was the home, in the mid 1860s, of William Coe and his gang of fifty to sixty rustlers and highwaymen.

The Coe men stole livestock, raided wagon trains on the Santa Fe Trail and committed other brands of mischief. Their hideout, north of

33

present Kenton and just outside the New Mexico line, was a large stone fort. It had walls thirty inches thick and loopholes to fire through. Inside, there was a barroom with a piano and dancing girls.

Coe, described as a stocky fellow with a moon face and bushy whiskers, was courteous in manner. He must have had an iron will to hold such a large gang under control. He was smart, too, but not smart enough to keep from making a fatal mistake. He set his men to robbing the horse herds at Fort Union in eastern New Mexico and Fort Lyon in Colorado. That brought the army upon him.

According to best reports Lieutenant Colonel William Penrose and a troop of soldiers swept down from Fort Lyon determined to put an end to Coe's activities once and for all. They carried a small cannon for use against the outlaw's fort.

Penrose first surprised eleven of the gang holed up in an outlying cabin. The men were all asleep, never dreaming that anyone would invade remote Robbers' Roost. They were captured without a struggle, taken to nearby cottonwoods and promptly hanged.

Next the troops descended on the stone fort. A furious battle followed that ended when a volley of shots from the cannon tore a hole in the walls. The defenders ran out like bees from an upturned hive. Many were gunned down, but others, including William Coe, scattered into the canyons.

Now the leader became a hunted man. A small detachment from Fort Union moved into the area and camped at the Madison Emery Ranch some miles east of the "Three Corners." The soldiers scoured the country for several days, but finding no trace of Coe, they moved on.

A few hours after their departure William Coe, looking starved and haggard, rode into the ranch. At that moment no one was home except Mrs. Emery and her young son. The outlaw asked for food and was fed. Then taking his rifle he went to the bunkhouse and tumbled into a bed for some much needed sleep.

Immediately, Mrs. Emery instructed her son to saddle his pony and ride like the wind after the soldiers. The hours dragged by as the terrified woman waited. She feared that Coe would awake, discover the boy missing and shoot her out of rage.

Finally the blue-coated men returned and surrounded the bunkhouse. William Coe was taken without a fight. As he was led away he gave Mrs. Emery a strange smile. The officer of the detachment remarked to her, "Ma'am, if that gent ever escapes, your life won't be worth a pinch of salt." But the brave lady was soon spared that worry.

Bandit Coe was taken to the town of Pueblo, Colorado, and lodged in jail. A few nights later a mob broke into the lock-up and carried him out, still handcuffed. In a short time he was left hanging from a tree along the banks of nearby Fountain Creek.

Decades later, workmen were clearing an area for the expansion of modern Pueblo. All at once their machinery unearthed a skeleton wearing handcuffs. Old-timers announced that it was the exact spot where William Coe had been hanged on the night of July 21, 1868.

San Francisco Street, Santa Fe, looking east. Sketched by Theodore R. Davis. (Neg. no. 31339, courtesy Museum of New Mexico.)

Chief Justice Slough Is Shot

Shootings and gun battles were commonplace in the turbulent days of the New Mexico Territory. Sometimes they developed into "wars" such as those in Lincoln and Colfax counties, which had dozens of participants and stretched over several years. But on most occasions, it was a simple and single incident of violence, as in the case of Colonel Albert Jennings Fountain. In 1896 he and his young son were ambushed and murdered somewhere in the White Sands by persons unknown.

There were also cases of the kind later made famous by Hollywood— two men meeting each other head on and shooting it out over some affair of honor or minor point of disagreement. We tend to think that such episodes were confined to drunken cowboys or professional gunslingers. In point of fact, they often involved prominent and respected men and produced what was known at the time as "high-class killings." The slaying of Judge John P. Slough in the old La Fonda Hotel on the Santa Fe Plaza must be regarded as one of the highest of that class.

A native of Ohio, Slough had gone to the newly organized Territory of Colorado in 1860 to practice law. When the Civil War broke out he organized a regiment of Union volunteers and marched south to defend New Mexico. Confederate troops, who had ridden up the Rio Grande from El Paso, were stopped by Colonel Slough's forces at the Battle of Glorieta Pass in late March of 1862.

Following this success, Slough was called to service in the East where he soon rose to the rank of Brigadier General. He distinguished himself during campaigns in the Shenandoah Valley and won appointment as military governor of Alexandria, Virginia. At the close of the war he was given the post of Chief Justice of the Territory of New Mexico.

With wife and children, Judge Slough took up residence in Santa Fe and entered wholeheartedly into his duties. A local newspaper described him as "a gentleman of high mental cultivation and unsurpassed social qualities, connected with an elevated sense of honor." The judge was a big man, over 200 pounds, and at this time, 1867, was in his late thirties. Evidently he was possessed of a quick temper and on occasion displayed an abrasive manner, for he soon developed bitter enemies in high political circles. Some of these he denounced publicly in language that was described as "more forcible than polite."

One of his leading foes was "Captain" W. L. Rynerson, a member of the Territorial Legislature representing Doña Ana County. Like Slough, Rynerson had originally come to New Mexico as a sergeant with the California Volunteers to defend the country from invading Confederates. Afterward he settled in the Mesilla Valley and entered politics. He was a sensitive, combative individual who often wore his long frock coat draped over his shoulders in the style of Count Dracula.

For reasons not clear Rynerson became the spokesman for those members of the Legislature who detested Judge Slough. Their power was sufficient to permit them to pass a resolution censuring the Chief Justice on charges of intimidating jurors, engaging in party politics and tampering with justice. They also got up a petition to Washington asking the President to remove him from office.

Matters came to a head on the afternoon of December 15 in the lobby of the Exchange Hotel, also known as La Fonda Americana. This was Santa Fe's most popular hostelry and the residence of Captain Rynerson when he was in town. Judge Slough was in the habit of drinking at the bar and shooting billiards there. On the evening of the fourteenth he had been heard to say over the billiard table that Rynerson was a liar and a thief. So when the two chanced to meet in the lobby on the following day the air was charged with electricity.

According to witnesses, Rynerson was stationed near the entrance of the bar wearing a Colt revolver which was only partially concealed by his loose coat. When the Judge entered he called to him in a loud voice, "I want you take it back."

Slough stopped, surprised, and said, "Take what back? What did I say?"

Rynerson replied, "You called me a thief and a liar."

And Slough answered, "I won't take it back."

At that point the Captain pulled his revolver and waved it menacingly in the air. "If you don't take it back," he announced calmly, "I'll shoot you."

Judge Slough placed his hand in his pocket and as he did so he said, "Shoot and be damned!"

Rynerson shot. The bullet struck its victim in the stomach. As Slough tumbled to the floor his hand came from the pocket and dropped a Derringer. Captain Rynerson appeared about to fire again, but a bystander shoved him through the doors of the bar and disarmed him.

Meantime friends had hurried to the fallen man's side. In a weak voice Judge Slough declared that he had been shot in the side and asked for someone to send for a doctor. Those were his last words.

The U.S. Marshall soon arrived and arrested Rynerson, placing him in the jail at Fort Marcy for safekeeping. The local paper announced the death of New Mexico's Chief Justice in a mournful obituary, lamenting, "In the prime of life and in the midst of a useful and honorable career he was struck down by the hand of violence." It was a familiar story in the Territory.

What happened to Captain Rynerson was also a familiar tale. He was granted a change of venue to Las Vegas and, standing trial, was acquitted on a plea of self-defense.

Today, La Fonda Hotel on the site of the old La Fonda Americana is thronged with guests who daily pass through the lobby, totally unaware that they are walking over the site of a tragic episode in New Mexico's history.

Badman Leyba

In Territorial days New Mexico had its full share and more of gunmen, road agents, and cattle rustlers. Outlaws chased from neighboring Texas, Colorado, Utah and Arizona often found sanctuary in New Mexico's small and lawless towns hidden away in the mountains and desert. Notorious names like Billy the Kid, Clay Allison, Black Jack Ketchum, and the Apache Kid grabbed the headlines, but there were plenty of others, not so famous, who helped fill out the lengthy roster of badmen. One was Marino Leyba, a native son of the Territory.

Leyba was tall, well over six feet, had steely blue eyes and sported a swooping handle bar mustache. His iron nerve was matched only by a surly disposition. Contemporary accounts say that his favorite prank was to terrorize small farming villages by riding at breakneck speed down the main street shooting off the heads of every chicken in sight.

Marino Leyba ranged wide across New Mexico, and he is credited with having at least one shooting scrape with Sheriff Pat Garrett on the Pecos River. But the center of his activity during the early 1880s was in the rough country north of the Sandia Mountains between Santa Fe and Albuquerque. The largest town in the area and his favorite hangout was the mining camp of Golden.

Western author Charles F. Lummis, passing through Golden, met Leyba in a saloon and had a friendly drink and chat with him. He described the outlaw as "ordinarily a good-natured fellow whose bravado was endless and covered no lack of courage." Only later did Lummis learn he had been associating with one of the Territory's most feared desperados.

Leyba had put together a gang of assorted cutthroats and with them waylaid travelers and stole livestock at every opportunity. In the fall of 1880, however, he committed a foul murder that eventually proved his undoing. The victim was Colonel Charles Potter, a U.S. geological surveyor, who had been sent by the government to study the mineral resources of New Mexico.

Potter arrived in Albuquerque in October, rented a horse and rode eastward into the Sandia Mountains to have a look at some new mining discoveries. Friends warned him that it was not safe to travel alone, but he paid no attention.

In Tijeras Canyon, alongside present Interstate 40, he stopped at a small shack to ask directions. The owner, a shady character named Cali-

41

fornia Joe, came out to speak to him. Unknown to Potter, Marino Leyba and his men at that moment were inside having a meal.

When the outlaws saw the prosperous looking Colonel through the window, they quickly hatched a plan. One of their number slipped outside and whispered to California Joe, instructing him to steer the traveler onto an isolated back trail. When he had gone the outlaws mounted up, followed a short cut and prepared an ambush. The unsuspecting Potter, riding leisurely along, was suddenly felled by a hail of bullets. Leyba and his companions stripped the body of valuables, piled logs over it and set it afire. Then they rode away chuckling over their good fortune.

The disappearance of Colonel Potter created a stir throughout New Mexico and even in Washington, since he had been a government employee. The investigation was placed in the hands of Albuquerque sheriff Perfecto Armijo, and local newspapers offered a large reward for clues.

Months passed and no leads surfaced. Then Sheriff Armijo got a break. Someone reported seeing a gold pocket watch in an Albuquerque pawn shop that resembled one known to have belonged to the missing Colonel.

Going to the shop, Armijo learned that the watch and chain had already been melted down for their gold. But the inner works had been saved along with a small picture that the case had held. The likeness was identified as Mrs. Potter.

Records showed that the man who pawned the watch was Pantaleon Miera, a resident of Bernalillo, twenty miles upriver. When the Sheriff went there he found that he was too late. Miera had been lynched by vigilantes a short time before for stealing a horse. But since he had been a known member of the Leyba gang Armijo felt certain that he now knew who was responsible for Colonel Potter's disappearance. He therefore issued warrants for the outlaw leader and his men.

One of the culprits was soon caught at nearby Isleta and taken to the Albuquerque jail. He was Escalastico Perea and under questioning he revealed the sordid details of the crime, including the location of the Colonel's body. With two deputies Sheriff Armijo rode into the Sandias to recover the remains. He also brought in two of Leyba's accomplices, one of them California Joe.

That night lynching talk was the main topic of conversation in most of Albuquerque's saloons. But a traveling minstrel show had scheduled a performance in the evening and the light-hearted entertainment, attended by a large crowd, seemed to dispel the atmosphere of violence. Appearances, however, proved deceiving.

At a late hour a mob of some two hundred men, their faces concealed by handkerchiefs, marched resolutely to the jail. The prisoners, struggling desperately, were carried outside and in the phrasing of the day were "launched into eternity."

Next morning, the people of Albuquerque awoke to a startling head-

Church at Golden, January 1972. Photograph by LeRoy D. Moloney. (Neg. no. 53194, courtesy Museum of New Mexico.)

line spread across the front page of the newspaper. Under the bold words "DANCING ON AIR" they read the details of the previous night's hanging. The mob, claimed the paper, had been composed mainly of Hispanos who had long suffered at the hands of the Leyba gang.

A few weeks later, another of the villains was captured. He too soon fell victim to the handiwork of the Albuquerque vigilantes. The *Santa Fe New Mexican* in an editorial placed its stamp of approval on the treatment accorded the killers: "Though lynching in general is to be condemned, yet to every case there is an exception which simply proves the rule. And in cases such as the cowardly and dastardly murder of Colonel Potter, it is very doubtful whether justice can be too swiftly meted out."

Only the leader Marino Leyba now remained at large. With four hangings already accomplished he decided the Territory was too hot for safety. He fled to Mexico where he stayed for several years.

Afterward, homesick for his old haunts, Leyba returned to Golden, organized a new gang and resumed his misbegotten ways. He was finally killed in a gunfight with lawmen in 1886.

Shoot-Out
at Estancia Spring

The New Mexico frontier a century ago was a violent place. Most men wore a six-gun belted to the waist and carried a rifle in their saddle scabbards. The handiness of such arms meant that a simple quarrel or the slightest disagreement could quickly become a shooting matter. Things were so bad that some dance hall keepers installed signs that read: "Please don't shoot the musicians. They're doing the best they can."

Of the great variety of controversies at that time none was more likely to lead to gunfire than the one involving conflicts over the old Spanish and Mexican land grants. In fact, the issue is still a hot one today and instances of violence are reported almost every year.

In the summer of 1883, feuding over grants got out of hand in the Estancia Valley between Albuquerque and Santa Rosa. Before it was over two men were dead and the Territory was in an uproar.

Back in 1819, when New Mexico was still part of the Spanish Empire, a man named Bartolomé Baca had applied for a grant of more than a million acres in the Estancia Valley. For some years Baca ran huge flocks of sheep on the grant, but for reasons lost to history, he appears to have neglected acquiring legal papers giving him final title to the princely ranch. After his death Baca's heirs sold their claim to the grant to the powerful Otero family who had a large hacienda on the Rio Grande near Los Lunas.

The year before New Mexico passed from Mexican to American rule, 1845, Governor Manuel Armijo made a new grant, consisting of 300,000 acres in the very center of the old Baca tract, to a rancher named Antonio Sandoval. This became known as the Estancia grant. Later Sandoval's nephew inherited the land and sold it in the early 1880s to a couple of millionaire brothers from Boston, Joel and James Whitney.

The scene was now set for trouble because both the Whitneys and the Oteros were claiming ownership of the heart of the Estancia Valley. Each side faced a tangle of legal problems and the matter finally went to the courts for decision.

The Boston brothers, however, were unwilling to await the outcome of a lengthy judicial review. James, the younger of the pair, set up headquarters in a house at Estancia Spring, hired a pack of cowboys and began pushing the Otero's sheepherders out of the valley.

In mid-August 1883, twenty-three-year-old Manuel B. Otero left his family's hacienda on the Rio Grande and rode east to force a showdown with the intruders. He was accompanied by his cousin Carlos Armijo and a Dr. Henríquez who was his brother-in-law. The men crossed the Manzano Mountains and descended to the valley beyond. On the way a traveler warned them that James Whitney was at Estancia Spring with seven men and was threatening to kill any Otero on sight.

At the ranch headquarters Manuel and his companions dismounted. They went to the door and barged into the front room. Whitney was there with his brother-in-law, Alexander Fernández, and another employee.

Sharp words followed and then all at once everyone had his pistol out and was blazing away. Fernández was killed instantly. James Whitney received a bullet in the jaw and Dr. Henríquez in the hand.

Manuel Otero, shot in the neck, staggered backward into the front yard with the smoking gun still in his hand. Cowboys who came running from the barn saw him collapse on the ground.

The small room was a shambles, its walls spattered with blood and the air thick with gunsmoke. James Whitney lay on the floor groaning horribly.

Dr. Henríquez, now that the fight was over, took charge. After bandaging his own hand, he had Otero brought inside and placed on a cot. The bullet had severed an artery in the young man's neck and he was bleeding profusely. The doctor did what he could to stop the flow. Then he tended to Whitney.

It was clear to all that Otero's hours were numbered and a rider was sent to the village of Manzano for a priest. After a bit Manuel was placed upon a mattress in a wagon and a slow start made on the road to Los Lunas. At sunset the priest caught up with the party, but it was too late. The wagon by that time was bearing a corpse.

James Whitney had also been placed in a wagon by his cowboys who rushed him to St. Vincent Hospital in Santa Fe. There, after stitching him back together, the doctors declared that he would recover. By a strange quirk of fate the nurse assigned to take care of him was María Otero, sister of the man Whitney had just killed.

The elder brother, Joel Whitney, when he heard of the affray rushed to Santa Fe in his private railroad car. In the middle of the night he entered St. Vincent's and had James carried to the train on a stretcher. Knowing that the entire Territory was outraged over the death of the popular young Otero, he feared his brother might be lynched.

The Whitneys got only as far as Las Vegas. Governor Lionel Sheldon, when he learned of their flight, wired the sheriff at Las Vegas and ordered him to stop the train and seize the two brothers.

The following April, 1884, James Whitney was brought to trial. By then tempers had cooled and the jury was able to consider the evidence rationally. Since all parties to the shooting had been armed, it was decided that it had been a fair fight and the defendant was acquitted.

The real tragedy of the affair did not become apparent until long afterward when the courts finally ruled on the land grants which had started the trouble. Both grants were declared to be invalid. The Estancia Valley was placed in the public domain and opened for homesteading.

So, the bloody shoot-out at Estancia Spring had all been for nothing!

Mystery of the Mayberry Murders

Murder and mayhem, crimes of passion and senseless brutality have been part of history since time began. They spring from the dark side of man—from that portion of the human equation that remains inexplicable.

In 1885, the beautiful little mining camp of Bonito City high among the pines between Carrizozo and Ruidoso was the last place one would have expected to hear of violence. There was a single saloon, which, though it catered to local miners, was a place of quiet recreation and decorum. There was a post office, a general store and a scattering of small residences all made of logs cut on the neighboring slopes above Bonito Creek.

And there was a two-story building, the hotel, operated by the Mayberry family. Mr. and Mrs. John Mayberry and their daughter Nellie had quarters on the ground floor, while upstairs were the room for two sons and the rooms for guests. Bonito City was off the beaten track and visitors were few. The Mayberrys made ends meet by opening their dining room to the miners who flocked in for the evening meal.

That fateful year of 1885, the hotel had two permanent guests. One was Dr. R. E. Flynn, a physician from Cincinnati, who, traveling about the West, had taken a liking to the calm of Bonito City. The other was Martin Nelson, a friendly young man, aged twenty-four, who was well-liked by the townspeople.

Late one night the peace of the community was shattered forever. Martin Nelson took a .38 caliber rifle and walked to the closed door of the Mayberry boys who were sleeping. At a loud knock, seventeen-year-old Johnny Mayberry woke up and called, "Who's there?" Receiving no answer he went to the door and opened it.

Martin Nelson shot him. Though badly wounded Johnny struggled with his assailant for possession of the gun. But a second shot ended his life. Eddie, the other son, was screaming in his bed. Another bullet killed him instantly.

Dr. Flynn, hearing the commotion and shots, rushed into the hall. He was quickly felled by a blast from Nelson's gun. Mr. Mayberry rushing up the stairs met the same fate.

Mrs. Mayberry and Nellie were next. The young girl dropped with a bullet in her side, apparently dead. The unfortunate Mrs. Mayberry received a wound in the chest but was able to flee. She ran in terror through the hotel, her bare feet leaving bloody footprints on the floor. Reaching a neighboring cabin she pounded in frenzy on the door, but the frightened residents would not let her in.

Nelson caught up with her then, finished her with another shot and threw her body into a nearby irrigation ditch. Then he went on a rampage through town.

The saloon keeper met him in the street and became the next victim. The same misfortune overtook the proprietor of the general store when he appeared on his porch with gun in hand.

Throughout the night the people of Bonito City cowered in their homes. With morning's light they emerged heavily armed. On the mountain side above they spotted Martin Nelson. He raised his rifle to fire at the town. But one of the men, a noted sharpshooter, fired first. The long shot hit its mark and the murderer tumbled in a heap, dead.

The sheriff of Lincoln County, John W. Poe, was summoned, but there was nothing at this point that the law could do. The town buried the seven victims in a row and placed the grave of Martin Nelson a short distance away.

Only one member of the Mayberry family survived. Poor Nellie recovered from the wound in her side and soon after left New Mexico forever. Rumor had it that she later married a prosperous rancher in Kansas, but try as she might, she was unable to shake off the bitter memory of the horrible episode that claimed her family.

Bonito City never recovered. From then on it was a haunted place. The hotel was closed and no one dared set foot inside. Passersby reported hearing moans and muffled shots issuing from the dark interior. Children on their way to school made a wide circle to avoid it.

A newspaper reporter, according to one tale, came to investigate the story and entered the hotel to make a tour. Onlookers saw him emerge moments later on a dead run, his face pale and frightened as if he had met the Devil.

The Southern Pacific Railroad sealed Bonito City's doom a few years later. It built a dam across the creek and the town went under water. Before that happened, all the buildings, including the Mayberry hotel, were dismantled. The bodies in the cemetery were moved to the community of Angus a few miles away.

So Bonito City is gone. But the mystery remains. To this day no one has ever been able to explain why young Martin Nelson went on his pointless shooting spree.

The First New Mexico Penitentiary

History is full of fables—stories that have been told so often they are universally believed even though they are not based on fact. In New Mexico, one of the most common fables, found in most school texts, goes like this:

In 1889 the Territorial Legislature created a number of public institutions and provided that they should be located in the leading towns. To Albuquerque went a liberal arts university; to Socorro, a school of mines; to Las Cruces, an agricultural and mechanical college; to Las Vegas, the insane asylum; and to Santa Fe, the first penitentiary. Santa Fe, so the story goes, could have had the university allotted to Albuquerque. Instead, it used its political pull to secure the prison. Businessmen in the capital believed that institution would prove more profitable to the local economy than a university. Only later did they realize their mistake.

The tale has been told so often—Santa Fe choosing the penitentiary instead of the university—that it has become something of a historical joke. But the real joke is that it did not happen that way at all. The university and the several colleges were founded by the legislature in 1889, it is true. But Santa Fe could not have used its political clout to grab the prison at that time because, as early newspaper accounts clearly show, the prison was already in existence, having been opened in the capital four years before.

The movement to obtain a penitentiary for New Mexico seems to have begun in 1883. Up to that time long-term prisoners had to be placed in institutions out of the territory, mainly in Kansas. But now New Mexico began to take steps to care for its own.

One suggestion bandied about was that a prison be built in the mining community of Cerrillos located twenty miles south of the capital. It was thought the convicts could be worked in the mines and not only earn their keep but make a profit for the government. In the final decision, however, a site was selected on the south side of Santa Fe, along the railroad tracks, just west of present Cordova Road and St. Francis Drive. A contract was signed for construciton of the penitentiary in August 1884.

Exactly one year later, the red brick building was completed and ready for occupancy. On the evening of August 6, a gala public reception was held inside the walls so that New Mexicans might inspect the new facility. Guests donned their finery and arrived in a long line of horse-drawn carriages. Said one news account: "From 8 to 10 o'clock the crowd poured into that magnificent structure until every chair in the place was held at a premium and the grand chapel hall was filled with gay promenaders."

Vases of flowers had been placed everywhere, and the U.S. infantry band played lively airs for dancing. On the second floor, twenty waiters in white aprons "went rushing to and fro like mad arranging four long tables at which the visitors were to feast later on in the evening." It was a strangely festive affair for a place built with such a somber purpose.

Four years later when the legislature passed the educational bill it probably decided to give the schools to other towns since Santa Fe already had the penitentiary. But plainly, the capital was not involved in any kind of deal whereby it took the prison over the university. How that story got started may be impossible to determine at this late date.

Incidentally, the prison completed in 1885 served New Mexico until June 1956. At that time a new and larger penitentiary was opened eight miles south of Santa Fe. It was touted as the most modern penal facility in the country. That was the one, of course, practically demolished in the 1981 riot.

Old state prison at Santa Fe, ca. 1900. (S. Loomis Collection, New Mexico State Records Center & Archives, Santa Fe.)

The Mysterious Guadalupes

It is a safe bet that the Guadalupe Mountains are known firsthand to fewer New Mexicans than any other range in the state. Tucked away in the southeastern part of New Mexico and straddling the Texas boundary, they remain isolated and untouristed.

The terrain is unbelievably rugged, from boulder strewn McKittrick Canyon to the soaring heights of Guadalupe Peak (8,751 feet), located just below the New Mexico line and the highest point in Texas. Summer hikers who are willing to brave rattlesnakes, prickly pear and catclaw penetrate the remote sections of the mountains, as do fall hunters in pursuit of the plentiful deer population. But that is about all. The higher Guadalupes are not designed for casual picknicking or for RV's loaded with conveniences.

Probably the first Spaniard to get a look at these mountains was Gaspar Castaño de Sosa who marched up the Pecos Valley in 1590. From elevations below modern Carlsbad he could see the dark line of the sierra on the west. But instead of turning aside to explore the heights he continued on northward.

Just which Spaniard named the Guadalupes is uncertain. One theory is that the mountains took their names from the Guadalupe Mission Church at El Paso del Norte, founded in the second half of the seventeenth century. Of course the title came originally from the Patroness of Mexico, the Virgin of Guadalupe.

At first there was little to attract settlers to these mountains. In spite of patches of ponderosa pine and Douglas fir and stands of alligator-bark juniper the crumpled slopes presented a bleak appearance. And then too, the canyons which seamed the east and west faces were long the haunts of the Mescalero Apache.

The Mescaleros were mainly a mountain people, although they were equally adept at getting along in the desert. For centuries their main home was around Sierra Blanca Peak near Ruidoso, but they ranged and camped down through the Sacramentos and Guadalupes. To these sanctuaries they would flee after raiding Spanish settlements in the El Paso Valley or waylaying caravans on the Camino Real.

When Americans occupied the Territory and in 1855 built Fort Stanton close to Lincoln, the Apache moved even deeper into their mountain retreats. U.S. troops following their trails nearly always quit when the tracks led upward toward the loftiest reaches of the Guadalupes. Matters were different, however, when the hostile Indians descended to the flats below. Lieutenant Howard Cushing showed that in 1869 when he attacked and dispersed a Mescalero camp at the base of the range just across the Texas line.

Legends that reach back almost four centuries tell of gold hidden in the fastness of the Guadalupe Mountains. Territorial governor Lew Wallace once claimed to have turned up a treasure document in the old palace on the Santa Fe plaza.

It revealed that in the years before the Indian revolt of 1680 a Pueblo tribesman had guided a Capitan Gavilán and thirty other Spaniards down to a fabulous gold deposit situated in an eastern spur of the Guadalupes. This spur, according to the yellowed document, was covered with volcanic ash, so Gavilán and his men called it the Sierra de Cenizas, meaning Ashes Mountain. After a little probing they hit pay dirt and went home loaded with gold nuggets and lumps of ore. But then the revolt came and the Spaniards were driven out of northern New Mexico. In the tumult the gold was forgotten.

Governor Wallace, who had mining investments around the Territory, evidently decided not to spend time searching for Gavilán's lost mine. But Ben Sublett did. He was a hardrock prospector who had spent a lifetime beating the Rockies for a streak of color. Now he fastened his attention on the Guadalupes.

Year after year, Sublett ventured into the mountains, driving a decrepit old buckboard pulled by a pair of underfed horses. He lived on beans, flour and coffee and spent his days scratching at the earth. Then one day he left the Guadalupes, went to a saloon in town and dumped a canvas poke of gold nuggets on the bar. Ben Sublett had struck it rich!

He was not a greedy man, so he only returned to his mine when money got low and he needed another thousand or two worth of nuggets. Dozens of men tried to follow him on those trips but he eluded them all.

More than once Ben announced aloud: "If anyone wants my mine, let him go out and hunt for it like I did. I'm going to carry the secret to my grave." And that is apparently what happened.

Many men have scoured the Guadalupe wilderness searching for Gavilán's gold and Ben Sublett's mine (they may, in fact, be one and the same). But to date, no one has made a major strike. The mountains are keeping old Ben's secret to themselves.

The Ordeal of Jane Wilson

How much can the human body and spirit endure? The people who pioneered the raw and savage Southwestern frontier often had occasion to find out. That was the case with sixteen-year-old Jane Wilson. If ever a person was born under an unlucky star it was poor Jane!

At age three, she migrated from her native Illinois to Missouri with her parents and nine brothers and sisters. There her father ran a ferry boat but as that proved unprofitable he later took the family to a farm in east Texas. The move was ill-fated. Within a short time the parents and three of the brothers had died. The oldest surviving son barely had time to distribute the remaining children among neighbors when he fell victim to a fever.

Frail Jane, orphaned at fifteen, saw her smaller sisters (one of whom was a dwarf) scattered to the winds. But things began to look up not long afterward. She married Jim Wilson, a farmer, who was only nineteen. "We knew but little of life for I was not yet 16," she said later. "I fear we were crazy in getting married while we were so young."

Times were hard in Texas. So Jim took his wife in 1853 and joined a wagon train heading for California's promised land. His father and three younger brothers were part of the same caravan.

Jim and his father apparently quarreled with other members in the party. Therefore, at El Paso they dropped out, intending to wait and join the next train heading west. During the delay, however, thieves made off with much of their property so that it was impossible to go on.

"We could do nothing now," reports Jane, "except make our way back to east Texas."

Scarcely had they left El Paso, however, when Mr. Wilson and Jim, having gone ahead to scout the road, were murdered by Mescalero Apaches. Jane was now a widow. She also was responsible for her three younger brothers-in-law.

They returned to El Paso and waited for a ride east. Within a few weeks prominent miller and freighter Simeon Hart announced he was heading in that direction. He agreed to take the Wilson youngsters with him. He had an ox train driven by five Americans and one Mexican teamster.

After weeks on the trail the small train neared Fort Phantom Hill in north-central Texas. At that point the American drivers stole most of the livestock and disappeared. Hart and the oldest Wilson boy went in pursuit. Jane, the two younger boys and the Mexican teamster remained with the wagons.

Suddenly a war party of Comanches appeared and surrounded them. The Mexican was stripped of his clothing and with hands tied was ordered to kneel on the ground. One of the warriors shot him, stabbed him several times with a large butcher knife and then scalped him, though he was still alive. The Comanche tied the fresh scalp to a stolen hat he was wearing.

Understandably, Jane declares: "I was stupefied with horror as I gazed on this spectacle, and supposed that my turn would come next. But the Indians, having plundered the wagons, mounted us on mules and took us away. As I left, I looked back and saw the poor Mexican weltering in his own blood and still breathing."

The teamster, in fact, got up and tried to walk to the fort. Shot, stabbed, scalped, he wandered in circles for five days without food, covering fifty miles. He was finally rescued by a cavalry patrol and survived. Were people tough in those days?

Captive Jane and the two boys were distributed as prizes to leading warriors. The lads were given bows and arrows. Their faces were painted and, as future warriors of the tribe, they were spared any cruelty. Not so the hapless Jane.

Her incredible nightmare had just begun. Over the next several weeks she was treated with the most ferocious savagery. She was stripped virtually naked and her beautiful, long hair was cut leaving her body and head exposed to the merciless sun. No food was given her for days on end, and little water to soothe her swollen tongue.

Several warriors and a squaw joined the traveling band. Jane notes that the squaw, from whom she might have expected some compassion, heaped new cruelties upon her. She was forced to ride an unbroken mule without a bridle. The Comanches spent the day on the march amusing themselves by frightening the mule. They would shake the Mexican's now dried scalp in its face and roar with laughter when Jane was thrown violently to the ground.

"I never saw them exhibit the first sign of pity towards me," the girl later claimed. "It made no difference how badly I was hurt, if I did not rise immediately and mount the animal which had just thrown me, they would apply their riding whips, gunstocks, or lariats to my unprotected body with great violence.

"The squaw also would help me to rise by wounding me with the point of a spear. You may understand why the Indians put me on the wild mule and caused me to be thrown so often, when I tell you I expected to become a mother in a few months. They understood my situation, but instead of softening their hearts it only made them more inhuman, and subjected me to greater sufferings."

The abuse, described in pages of graphic detail, and her pregnancy took from the pathetic captive all will to live, or so she stated. But Jane Wilson came from solid pioneer stock, and when the chance arose to

Unidentified Comanche men. Photograph by Addison. (Neg. no. 2508, courtesy Museum of New Mexico.)

escape she seized it. Unguarded for a while, she crept away and hid in deep bushes. The Comanches, assuming she had crawled off to die, spent little time in search.

"My situation was now distressing beyond all description," Jane continued. "I was alone in Indian country, hundreds of miles from the nearest settlement and without food, shelter, or clothing. My body was full of wounds and bruises and wolves were all around me. Winter was coming on and death in its most horrible forms stared me in the face.

"But I could not weep; my heart was too full of woe. So I resolved to live in hope, even if I died in despair."

Perhaps it was that decision that finally turned Jane's luck around. After twelve days alone, eating nothing but hackberries, she was found by a party of traders and buffalo hunters from northern New Mexico. Her location then was somewhere on the high plains along the Texas-New Mexico border.

The New Mexicans had an uneasy truce with the Comanches allowing them to make quick trips to the plains. They took Jane, almost a walking skeleton, into their midst and treated her with great kindness. But soon their scouts announced that the Comanches were approaching.

One member of the group, a Pueblo Indian from San Ildefonso, led Jane away from camp, gave her several loaves of bread and hid her in a ravine. "To him more than any other man in the party," she later testified, "I owe my freedom."

For eight days the girl lay hidden. Rain beat down on her in prolonged spells and she trembled in terror lest the Comanches find her or the New Mexicans abandon her. But in the end the Indians left and her friends returned. Carried back to Santa Fe, her story of horror was shortly spread across the newspapers of the country.

The two Wilson lads captured with Jane were eventually ransomed at Fort Arbuckle in the Indian Territory (now Oklahoma). And Jane herself? Practically nothing is known of her life after the dreadful ordeal with the Comanches except for a single fact: Early in 1854, a frontier newspaper reported that miraculously Mrs. Jane Wilson had given birth to a fine boy. From that we can assume that her fortunes were finally looking up!

The Fate of Charlie McComas

Little blue-eyed Charlie McComas was six years old when he witnessed the killing of his parents by an Apache war party. The tragedy, one of New Mexico's biggest news stories of the day, occurred on March 28, 1883, a short distance north of Lordsburg along the Silver City road.

Judge H. C. McComas was one of the most prominent men in the Territory. Heavily burdened and wearing a fashionable frock coat, he had become a familiar sight on the streets of Silver City where he made his home. Mrs. McComas, a polished and cultured lady, came from an old Kansas family. Her brother was Eugene F. Ware, a popular poet who wrote under the name "Ironquill."

The judge had business at the mining camp of Leitendorf near Lordsburg. The weather was mild and thinking that his wife and young son Charlie would enjoy an outing in the buckboard, he took them along. Apache troubles had subsided of late; there seemed to be no danger.

Unknown to the McComas's, however, a sub-chief named Chato had broken loose from the San Carlos Reservation across the border in Arizona and with twenty-six men was cutting a bloody path southward toward Mexico. The raiders, armed with the latest model Winchester rifles, planned to join Geronimo's band, then hiding out in the Sierra Madre Mountains.

In Thompson's Canyon the Apaches, who had made a swing to the east, happened upon the luckless family. The startled judge made a quick U-turn with the buckboard. He handed the reins to his terrified wife, indicating that she should flee over their back trail. Taking his rifle he leaped to the ground to try to hold the attackers at bay. Making his stand by a small clump of bushes, he fired as fast as he could pump cartridges into the chamber. A volley of bullets, seven of which struck him square, ended Judge McComas's gallant defense.

Mrs. McComas fared no better. Fifty yards from where her husband had left them one of the horses was shot and dropped in the road. Thereupon the frantic mother grabbed her child and attempted to escape by running afoot. A warrior who dashed up behind crushed her skull with a rifle stock. Little Charlie was snatched from her lifeless arms and carried away.

Photograph on flyer announcing "Charley W. McComas: Captured by Indians." (From Emma Marble Muir, *Pioneer Schools*, 1957.)

These mournful details were pieced together by Jim Baker, driver of the stagecoach that came upon the grisly scene a few hours later. Without sparing the whip he raced his horses to the nearest ranch to spread the word.

The dreadful news made headlines across the nation. Not only had the victims been well-known, but the uncertain fate of the small boy added an element of high drama. Was he still alive? If so, could he be rescued?

Almost at once posses were formed. The Army was notified, and Captain James Black of the New Mexico Rangers sent out a squad to try and pick up the marauders' trail. For weeks men scoured the hills and desert basins. Photographs of Charlie with offers of a large reward were posted throughout southern New Mexico, Arizona and the north Mexican states, but all to no avail. He and the band of warriors had vanished into the forbidding precincts of the Sierra Madres.

The following May, General George Crook took advantage of a new international treaty that permitted U.S. troops to pursue hostile Indians into Mexico and headed into the mountains below the boundary. His main purpose was to round up the "bronco" Apaches who had found refuge there, but he also hoped to get a line on Charlie McComas. At mid-month the soldiers stormed and captured the main Apache rancheria high in the sierras. Shortly afterward Geronimo, Chato and other leaders came in from outlying camps and surrendered. But what of Charlie?

General Crook made inquiries of the captives. They told him that during the fight at the rancheria the frightened boy had fled into the woods and either starved or was killed. They professed to know nothing more. Crook so stated in his official report of the campaign.

Nevertheless, many people continued to believe that the full story of Charlie's end had not been told. The Apaches themselves for decades afterward remained close-mouthed about the affair, knowing the anger it caused among the Whites. Well into the twentieth century, old-timers among the Indians did divulge various conflicting details. Some said that little Charlie escaped with a few of the women when General Crook attacked their rancheria. Others claimed that the boy had been slain by a stray bullet.

The most solid account was given in 1959 by Jason Betzinez, who as a youth had been with the Apaches in Mexico. Betzinez created a sensation when, in his late nineties, he flew to New York to appear on the show "I've Got A Secret." His "secret" was the same as the title of his published autobiography, I Fought With Geronimo.

In that book he revealed the manner of Charlie McComas's death as it had been related to him years before by an eyewitness. When the soldiers struck the Apache camp a chance bullet had killed an old woman, mother of an Indian named Speedy. The warrior was so enraged that he snatched up a rock and brained poor Charlie who happened to be standing nearby. Betzinez declared that the truth could at last be told, since all concerned with the tragedy were now dead. (Ironically, after surviving the hazards of frontier warfare, Betzinez died in an automobile accident at age 101.)

The mystery of Charlie McComas seemed to have been put to rest. Yet there exists another possibility, one which will probably never be satisfactorily resolved. Some of those Apaches who asserted that Charlie had not been slain in the Sierra Madre fight stated that in fact they had seen him later in the company of "broncos" still hiding in the mountains long after Crook had departed.

In April 1930 a news dispatch carried by the United States press reported that a party of these aging "broncos" had raided a settlement in northern Sonora just below the Arizona border and had killed and scalped three persons. Eight years later an archeological expedition suddenly came upon this Indian remnant far up in the Sierra Madre. From a brief glimpse before the strange people disappeared the scholars observed that the leader had blue eyes and red hair! Their discovery rekindled speculation about Charlie McComas: as improbable as it appeared, could he have lived to become the last chief of the last free Apaches?

The Agony of
Jimmy McKinn

It was a warm September day in 1885 when ten-year-old Jimmy McKinn and his older brother Martin left their parents' ranch house near the Mimbres River east of Silver City to go bring in the cows. The two lads, sons of an Irish father and Mexican mother, were sturdy frontier types, used to their share of hard chores.

Not finding any stock, the boys split up to search a wider area. Suddenly young Jimmy heard piercing yells. In the distance he saw Martin surrounded by hostile Apaches. As he watched horrified, his blood turning to icewater, the Indians killed his brother and stripped the clothes off his body.

Jimmy scampered for cover, concealing himself in thick brush, but the war party had already spotted him. In a matter of minutes he was a captive. Roughly thrust upon a horse behind a broad-shouldered warrior, his ordeal began.

The Indians, the boy soon learned, were led by the most feared raider in the Southwest, Geronimo. With his small band he had broken away from a reservation in Arizona Territory and was on his way to sanctuary in the rugged mountains of northern Mexico. Along the trail the Apaches were pausing long enough to commit what mischief they could.

For two days and nights the party with little Jimmy in tow traveled without rest or sleep. Exhausted and famished, he held on to his captor with a death grip, fearful of falling from the horse. Once some of the band broke off and rounded up loose cattle, intending to drive them back to camp for food, but a posse of cowboys intercepted them, recaptured the stolen stock and shot one of the Apaches.

Finally the Indians killed one of their own horses and feasted on its flesh. Jimmy ate with as much appetite as anyone else. The meal helped restore his strength. But as to where he was, or where he was being taken, he had no idea.

At one point, perhaps near Deming, his Indian companions attacked a frame store, looted it of flour, sugar, molasses, and bacon, and then left the building in flames. Later they killed a teamster on the road and from his wagon made off with a huge quantity of candy.

Days afterward the Apaches reached a camp in the mountains of

Mexico where they were joined by some of their women and children. There Jimmy was put to work carrying firewood and herding horses. At first the Indians spoke to him in Spanish (his mother's tongue, which he understood perfectly). They called him Santiago—which is Spanish for James. But very quickly the boy began to master the language of the Apaches.

In spite of the hardships he adapted to his new life well and came to enjoy the rough and tumble ways of the Apache youngsters. Even the smaller Indian boys had the skills of warriors, and they carried rifles and wore belts of ammunition across their chests.

As months went by tension increased in the camp. The Apaches were being hounded from all sides. Mexican troops were in the field against them, and their scouts reported that an American army under their old foe General George Crook had moved below the border to seek them out.

This bad news put Geronimo in a surly mood. One day in a fit of anger he struck Jimmy (or Santiago) on the side of the head with his gun. The poor lad was knocked flat and suffered a severe injury. After that he made a resolution to stay out of Geronimo's way.

But the free days of the Apaches were numbered. Crook was closing in and they had already received a message from him that he wanted to parley to set terms for surrender. Geronimo, seeing the handwriting on the wall, agreed.

Among the peace delegation that soon came to the Indian camp was Crook, Lieutenant John G. Bourke and famed photographer C. S. Fly. Bourke, who later wrote of his frontier experiences, tells how surprised they were to see "among the group of little Apache boys romping freely and carelessly together" one who was pale and fair. After some persuasion he finally told the soldier in Spanish that his name was Santiago McKinn and that he had been captured at Mimbres, New Mexico.

"He seemed to be kindly treated by his young campanions," Bourke relates, "and there was no interference with our talk. He was about ten years old, slim, straight, and sinewy, blue-gray eyes, badly freckled, light eyebrows and lashes, much tanned and blistered by the sun, and wore an old once-white handkerchief on his head which covered it so tightly that the hair could not be seen."

Blond little Santiago amid the dark-hued Indian children was a photographer's subject made to order. Mr. Fly boldly toted his heavy box camera among the frowning Apaches and snapped a rare shot of a captive among his captors.

During the negotiations Geronimo agreed to lead his people back across the border escorted by Crook's men. On the journey Santiago, by his own wish it appears, remained with the Indians. When they all reached Fort Bowie in the southeast corner of Arizona Charles Lummis, a war correspondent for the *Los Angeles Times*, recounted what happened next:

"Santiago McKinn, this poor child, scaly with dirt, wild as a coyote,

Apache captive Jimmy (Santiago) McKinn. Photograph by C. S. Fly. (Neg. no. 11649, courtesy Museum of New Mexico.)

made my eyes a bit damp. His is a pathetic case. The sorrow of it is that he has become so absolutely Indianized. He understands English and Spanish, but it was like pulling eye-teeth to get him to speak either. He has learned the Apache language and talks it exclusively. When told that he was to be taken back to his father and mother, Santiago began boo-hooing with great vigor. He said in Apache that he didn't want to go back; he wanted always to stay with the Indians. All sorts of rosy pictures of his home were drawn, but he would have none of them, and acted like a young wild animal in a trap. When they lifted him into the wagon, he renewed his wails, and was still at them as he disappeared from our view."

Santiago was met by his father in Deming and was taken on the train to Silver City. When they arrived a large crowd was waiting on the platform and the boy discovered that he was a celebrity. Reporters for the *Silver City Enterprise* got his story, but all in Spanish, for he still refused to have anything to do with English.

Speaking of the interview and the throng of curious people the *Enterprise* noted in its pages that Jimmy McKinn was "the lion of the hour." Also, it editorialized: "He will make a good witness against Geronimo, as he saw him kill his brother. Much valuable information could be obtained from the boy if time was taken to question him closely by a person familiar with the Spanish language."

That was wishful thinking on the part of the newspaper. Even if the opportunity had arisen it seems unlikely that Jimmy would have been willing to testify against his Indian friends or give information harmful to them.

In Silver City the boy and his father climbed aboard a stagecoach and headed for home on the Mimbres River. As they neared his house, Jimmy borrowed Mr. McKinn's gun and fired it in the air, announcing their arrival and the end of his long ordeal.

Later in life Jimmy McKinn grew a red beard, became a blacksmith, married and raised a family. In 1908 it is known that he was the smith for the W. A. Tenney Freight Company in Silver City. Afterward he moved to Phoenix where he died in the mid-1950s.

In his last years McKinn was not eager to talk about his boyhood episode among the Indians. One of his sons married a Chiricahua Apache, and although Jimmy could speak to her in her own language there was always a tone of hostility in his voice. The painful experience of his youth left its mark upon him to the end of his life.

The W S Ranch and the Last Apache Uprising

One of New Mexico's most famous old-time cattle outfits was the huge W S Ranch founded in 1882. Its headquarters was on the San Francisco River about eighty miles northwest of Silver City and not far from the mining community of Alma. Harold C. Wilson of Cheltenham, England, owned the ranch, but the man who put it together and served as the first general manager was a youthful frontiersman named James H. Cook.

Born in Michigan in 1857, Cook had gone west as a teenager to become a cowboy. Landing in south Texas, he went to work on the famous Slaughter Ranch and cut his teeth on half a dozen long drives to the cattle towns of Kansas. Along the way he developed an affection for hunting. Those were the days when the western prairies and mountains teemed with game and any marksman could bag whatever he wanted.

Drifting up to Cheyenne, Wyoming, James Cook got a job supplying venison and antelope to a large hotel by the railroad depot. Soon he branched out and was guiding hunting parties into the Bighorn Mountains along the Montana border. Among the sportsmen were a number of Englishmen out for a frolic in America's Wild West.

"They were Oxford men," Cook said, "athletic, full of life and with all the education necessary to make anyone fully enjoy living close to Mother Nature. They remained in camp about a month and returned to England fully loaded with trophies."

Young Cook's fame as a skillful guide spread among Britishers and he had all the business he could handle. Many of his clients were members of the titled nobility. Thus it was that in the fall of 1882, after a particularly successful hunt in the Bighorns, Harold Wilson and several of his friends asked their guide for advice on buying ranches in the West.

James Cook declared that once on a hunting trip in southern New Mexico he had spotted some prime grazing country along the Gila River and its tributaries. If a fellow was starting from scratch and had plenty of capital, that was the place to go, he advised.

The men from England agreed and Wilson himself hired Cook on the spot to go select the land and put the ranch in operation. In a matter of months house and corrals were built and cowboys hired, and cattle grazed the vast pastures of the new W S Ranch. Other Englishmen in the group developed large properties within a fifty-mile radius, and all

69

Chiricahua Apache leader Geronimo, taken before his surrender. (Neg. no.
2115, courtesy Museum of New Mexico.)

sought the management advice of twenty-five-year-old James Cook.

The railway point nearest the W S headquarters was at Deming, but supplies freighted from there could be purchased at Silver City. Mail was brought there by a six-horse Wells Fargo Stage. A shotgun guard regularly rode on the box, for that part of New Mexico was infested with outlaws.

The novice Englishmen soon discovered that there were dangers more fearsome than desperados. In the summer of 1885 the most dreaded Indian in the Southwest, Geronimo, broke from his reservation in Arizona and with a band of renegades crossed the line into New Mexico. At the time, James Cook was entertaining a Mr. Lyon from England who, like his fellow countrymen, was considering investing in the area. He had been staying at the neighboring S U ranch and shortly before he was scheduled to start his long trip home had come over to the W S to go quail hunting with Cook.

When their excursion was finished Lyon bid the manager goodby and headed his horse up the trail to the S U. A half hour later, a rider on a lathered horse thundered into headquarters with the news that Geronimo's Apaches were sweeping the country. At least one party of travelers was known to have been slaughtered.

Most of the cowboys were gone on a round-up and Cook was at the ranch house with only a housekeeper and a retired hand, Charlie Moore. The three of them fortified the house with sandbags, anticipating an attack.

No attack came, but five citizens from Alma rode through on their way to check on the seriousness of the uprising. A few hours later one of their horses, riderless, galloped into the W S yard. The saddle was covered with blood, so Cook knew they had encountered Indians.

Shortly, a troop of cavalry and scouts under Lieutenant Charles Gatewood appeared. They were from Fort Apache, Arizona, and were hot on the trail of the renegades. As they wolfed down a meal served them in the ranch kitchen, they spoke grimly of the bodies of victims they had found and buried along the way.

Someone was needed to carry a message to Fort Bayard east of Silver City to alert the troops there and urge them to intercept the Apaches if they moved in that direction. Gatewood's men and horses were worn to the nub and that left James Cook to make the trip. Promptly he volunteered.

He left the ranch near sundown, rode all night, and reached the fort soon after dawn. He had covered just over one hundred miles in twelve hours. An incredible ride!

"That morning," he wrote in his memoirs long afterward, "the Indians killed a number of persons within three miles of both Fort Bayard and Silver City. Sixteen in all was the number, several of them being women and children. One or two of the children were tortured to death by being hung up on spikes outside their houses."

A report was received that a merchant driving a freight wagon to

Alma had been slain by Geronimo's warriors. Cook rode with the soldiers who went to check on the story. They picked up the Indian trail which was easy to follow because looted candy was spread along the way. Some of the sweets were of a kind then called "heart mottoes." The pieces had words written on them: "I Love You," "Kiss Me," and "You Are My Honey."

At one point the trackers found a large bar of perfumed toilet soap. Some warrior had mistaken it for a chunk of candy. There were teeth marks in it and also a large dent, showing that it had been hurled against a sharp rock. The trail soon fizzled out and a weary Cook left the troopers and headed home.

Back at the ranch, he received disturbing news. Mr. Lyon, his quail hunting companion, had never made it back to the S U Ranch. Some of the Englishmen from there were beginning a search, assuming that the Apaches had killed him.

Cook joined the group and they soon discovered Lyon's corpse. He had been ambushed and fallen in the trail. The Apaches had taken his gun and horse, but being in a hurry failed to scalp or mutilate him.

Reading sign, James Cook determined that the poor man had been jogging along reading a letter from home. Doubtless his mind was three thousand miles away in sunny England when fate intervened and the Apaches unleashed their arrows. Now he would remain in America for good—deep in a lonely grave in one of the wildest corners of New Mexico.

Stalking Grizzlies

Montague Stevens was an Englishman born with the itch to hunt. In the 1870s he accompanied several other British sportsmen to Wyoming in pursuit of big game. Later, hearing that hunting was superb in western New Mexico, he showed up in Socorro County, where deer, bear and mountain lion were so plentiful that he knew he had found a land of heart's delight.

At Horse Springs, over toward the Arizona line, Stevens picked up a cattle ranch and settled in to stay. Not long afterward he was visited by General Nelson A. Miles who was scouting the Territory at the very end of the Apache wars. With the Miles party was famed western artist Frederic Remington, on the lookout for dramatic scenes to paint.

On Stevens' ranch Remington wrote: "His door-yard is some hundreds of miles of mountain wilderness and desolate mesa—with its plains dotted with antelope and its mountains filled with cougar, deer, bear, and wild turkeys. The owner attends to the rounding-up of his cattle, but he does not let that interfere with the time all Englishmen set apart to be devoted to sport."

The artist went on to describe Montague as "a tall, thin young man, very much bronzed, and wearing corduroy clothes." Then he noted the strangest thing about him. His left arm was missing.

The arm had been lost years before in a hunting accident. Montague recorded the details afterward in his memoirs: "While hunting wild geese in California, and riding a friend's horse, I had a loaded shotgun in front of me, laid across the saddle. Suddenly the horse bolted. I grabbed the muzzle of the gun with my left hand while I tried to pull up the horse with my right. A branch caught the hammer, jerking the gun around, when it went off and blew my arm to pieces."

Apparently the mishap did not keep him from hunting. As he tells us: "Since the accident it was awkward for me to handle a rifle properly. But I have managed to get along, though it is somewhat of a handicap in an emergency. And when shooting grizzlies at close quarters in dense brush, emergencies are not infrequent."

Hunting bears with a good pack of dogs was Montague Stevens' passion in life. He also regarded it as something of a necessity since the animals killed hundreds of dollars worth of his livestock every year.

Whenever his neighbors started losing stock to a bear marauder they always called in Montague to solve the problem.

One large bear that eluded him for years he called the Jewett Gap grizzly. It had become famous in Socorro County for all the damage caused. Large bounties had been offered and many able hunters had followed the creature's track. But still it roamed free.

Montague Stevens and companion with dead bear. (From Montague Stevens, *Meet Mr. Grizzly*, 1944.)

One day Stevens got word that the Jewett Gap grizzly had just run through a flock of sheep, killing about forty and carrying one two miles before eating it. Saddling up and turning his hounds loose, he took up the trail.

A few hours later, he ran on a freshly killed cow with its neck broken. Here the bear had eaten dinner. A few miles beyond the dogs jumped the grizzly, who had bedded down for the night.

Stevens chased it into some timber and got it cornered. With one arm he raised the rifle and fired at the bear's throat. At that instant the animal raised a foreleg to swat at the dogs and took the shot in the paw. Then he sprinted straight for the hunter.

Struggling to cock his rifle Montague looked up to find the gaping jaws of the grizzly almost upon him. At the last possible moment he fired, breaking the bear's backbone and sending him rolling over and over downhill.

"Incidents such as that," he declared later, "have a tendency to undermine one's self-confidence, and self-confidence is an indispensible requisite in hunting grizzlies!"

In 1896 all the ranch country was astir when it was learned that Montague Stevens had taken a bride. She was his childhood flame, a lady of good birth who had come all the way from England to start a new life in the wilds of New Mexico. The young lady arrived wearing the latest London fashions and bringing boxes of tapestries, silver plate and other luxuries to adorn the crude log ranch house.

Agnes Morley Cleaveland was the lady's nearest neighbor—seventy-five miles away. Being curious she decided to pay a social call. When she arrived by buckboard she found the new Mrs. Stevens in fancy dress out in the yard washing clothes in a tin tub.

Montague was away on a round-up, she explained. And the house-keeper that had been hired for her had suddenly quit. The lady had said to her innocently, "We'll not dine until your master arrives." And the maid replied, "I'll have you know I ain't got no master." Then she whipped off her apron and promptly departed the ranch.

"One doesn't say things like that in Socorro County," Mrs. Cleaveland gently advised her hostess.

Later they went inside while Montague's wife prepared a meal. With the maid gone, an old white-haired cowboy came from the bunkhouse to assist her. Working hard she fixed imported curry from India and opened a rare wine. The food was placed in a fancy serving dish.

One thing was missing from the meal—tomatoes. The cowboy brought a can from the pantry, picked up an ax from the corner and used it to cut the top off. Then he set the tomato can with its jagged edges in the center of the elegant table. Mrs. Stevens never blinked an eye. She was learning what it was like to be living in the house of a rough bear hunter and rancher.

A Bloodthirsty Family

In the summer of 1891 a prominent jeweler from Boston, Campbell Hardy, happened to be in Chicago on business. A young newspaper reporter, learning that he had once been a traveling peddler in the wild Southwestern territories, asked Mr. Hardy to relate his most memorable experience.

The dapper jeweler responded with a chilling tale that he claimed had actually happened some ten years before in the mountains of southern New Mexico. At that time peddlers commonly wandered up and down the Rio Grande Valley and across the desert basins between the Sacramento Mountains on the east and the Black Range on the west. With their small stock of goods packed on a burro or sometimes in a wagon they were welcome visitors in small towns and at isolated farms and ranches.

One day about noon Hardy had drawn up at a ramshackle cabin on the pine-clad slope of a mountain. He was carrying about $800 worth of stock plus some $1,200 in cash. Being tired and hungry he asked for lunch. Invited inside, he discovered the occupants of the place were a sour-looking man of about sixty, his twenty-five-year-old son and two women, who he guessed to be wives of the men.

The disagreeable appearance of his rough-looking hosts made Campbell Hardy sorely regret that he had stopped here. The women, as usual, wanted to see what he had for sale. He pulled out a few things, and they purchased about three dollars' worth.

The old man, whose name was Moody, kept asking probing questions: Had the peddler seen anybody on the trail recently? Did he have any friends in this part of the country? In view of what followed Hardy afterward expressed the belief that the rascal was trying to find out if anyone would miss him if he was murdered.

As he was sitting down at the lunch table the peddler happened to glance out of the window. He caught sight of the son, who had gone out earlier, carrying a shotgun toward the barn. His stealthy manner immediatley put Hardy on guard. As fast as possible, he choked down his coffee and bread and got up to leave.

"But you must come in the barn and see my blooded horses," Moody said. "Likely, I can trade one for a silver watch, or something else you have in your pack."

Knowing of a certainty that if he ever went in that barn he would never come out again, Mr. Hardy made several weak excuses and turned to ride away. As he did the man became enraged and hurled curses at him.

Gaining shelter in the trees, the traveler reined up and peered back at the barn. Father and son soon emerged, both carrying guns, and started along the road. It was evident they were going out to prepare an ambush for their recent guest.

Instead of continuing ahead Hardy wheeled around and went as fast as he could in the opposite direction. About a half mile from the cabin he ran into two honest-looking trappers and related the details of his narrow escape.

"I always believed that old wretch was a murderer," commented one of the men. They then offered to go back and confront Moody.

But Hardy was not looking for adventure and he declined their suggestion. However, since the pair was armed with rifles he offered them a silver watch as payment if they would accompany him a ways and provide protection.

About mid-afternoon a bullet came whizzing past Hardy's head and he jumped behind a tree as his companions slipped into the brush. Moments passed; shots rang out and the trappers called him to come ahead. Behind a log lay Moody and his son, shot dead.

The three then mounted up and returned to the cabin. Finding it empty, they looked into the barn and discovered the two women in a cellar under the building, digging a grave for Hardy.

When law officers were summoned, twenty skeletons were unearthed on the grounds. For several years Moody had been killing every stranger who dropped by. Before departing for the East Hardy had the satisfaction of hearing that the women had been hung for their part in the crimes.

As he approvingly told the young reporter in Chicago, "Moody's remains and those of his son were also hung on a tree near the side of the road, as a warning to murderers. That's how they do things out in New Mexico."

Shakespeare, New Mexico. (Neg. no. 55364, courtesy Museum of New Mexico.)

Rambles on the Southwestern Frontier

In 1928 retired Judge O. W. Williams of Fort Stockton, Texas, put down on paper recollections of his experiences on the New Mexico frontier almost fifty years before. While containing no earth-shaking revelations, his words do provide an interesting glimpse of life in the two mining camps of Carbonateville and Shakespeare.

As a youth Williams had graduated from Harvard Law School in 1876 and set up a practice in Chicago. But soon finding that he had lung trouble, he took his doctor's advice and headed for the arid Southwest. Landing in Dallas, he discovered that the town of 2500 people was already overstocked with lawyers. So he turned his interest to mining speculation.

Hearing of a new boom in Leadville, Colorado, he enlisted the company of several friends to ride there horseback. One of the men was J. W. Bell, an ex-Texas Ranger. Commented Williams long afterward, "For Bell the fates began here to spin a thread of life with an evil ending. He was killed by Billy the Kid at the LIncoln County Courthouse two years later."

After a hard journey the party reached the wild cowtown of Tascosa in the Texas Panhandle. Here they had news of a mining discovery in the Cerrillos Hills below Santa Fe. "As a result of this information," Williams notes, "we changed our plans and made New Mexico our destination."

Arriving at the boom camp of Carbonateville about fifteen miles south of Santa Fe, the group disbanded. Williams and Bell stayed through the summer staking claims that in the end proved not very prosperous.

"Every Sunday or two," O. W. Williams tells us, "Governor Lew Wallace would come out from Santa Fe in his ambulance (a popular excursion vehicle in that day) and spend time with the miners. He was a very democratic, sociable man, greatly liked by all. Those Sundays were red letter days to us. I have been told since that at that very time he was engaged in writing *Ben Hur*."

For recreation Williams occasionally visited Santa Fe. Since the majority of the people spoke only Spanish, he spent much of his time trying to communicate in sign language. But there were pleasures to be had. The Fort Marcy army band played weekly on the plaza and a dance,

81

or *baile,* could be found most nights.

"The belles of the Ball," says Williams, "came out in lace, black mantillas, and artificial flowers of colors and shapes never designed by nature."

Since his claims at Carbonateville were going nowhere he decided to give them up. By fall of 1879 he heard of a more promising camp opening in the southwest corner of the Territory at Shakespeare. Williams then grubstaked two broke prospectors named Grady and Pettie to go there and act as his agents.

The pair wanted to take along a third man—tall, blond William Tettenborn whose parents had come to the U.S. from Russia. Williams learned that the stranger had been in a gunfight in Fort Worth and a knife duel in Denver, and therefore he wanted no part of him. Tettenborn went south anyway where he became an outlaw under the alias "Russian Bill." He was later arrested for horse stealing and hanged from a rafter in a Shakespeare saloon.

After giving his agents instructions and sending them on their way, Williams returned to Texas on business and to spend the winter. His return to New Mexico the following spring was made by lurching stagecoach, via Fort Worth, San Angelo, Fort Stockton and El Paso. At the latter place he stopped over briefly at an adobe hotel next to the stage corral. El Pasoans were then much excited over the approach of two railroads, and Williams declares with astonishment that downtown property was selling "at the exorbitant price of $100 a lot."

Continuing on to Mesilla, he changed coaches for Silver City and Shakespeare. The passengers were all frightened with dire warnings of Apache attack. Halfway to Fort Cummings (northeast of present Deming), they encountered dead oxen and burned out freight wagons. A little beyond was a curious sight: stamped envelopes stuck to the tops of dry yucca stems, leading in a straight line across the desert.

At Fort Cummings they learned what the mystery was all about. Earlier a mail rider had been attacked and slain. A cavalry troop had gone out, found the trail of envelopes and followed them straight into an Apache ambush. Said Williams: "This was the purpose of the white markers and indicated considerable ingenuity on the part of the Indians."

At Silver City, which he described as "the most substantially built of all territorial towns outside Santa Fe," Williams changed stages again. This one took him to his final destination, Shakespeare, near the Pyramid Hills.

At this time the town's population was about 150, but fully one third of that number were prospectors and ranchers who had come in to escape the Indian threat. Smoke signals were seen daily on the distant mountain tops.

Williams learned that Apaches had already killed one of his prospectors, Grady, but the other, Pettie, had managed to stake several claims. That was enough to keep him in the area for the rest of the year. However, this mining venture, like the earlier one at Carbonateville, finally failed.

All that O. W. Williams got for his pains was a firsthand view of rough life on New Mexico's last frontier. In his old age he would say: "I'm astonished even yet to consider the enormous waste of time, money and life in the Territory, due to the evils of gambling and drinking. When I once asked an old time miner from Shakespeare if he drank in the early days, he replied, 'Never! And that's why I'm still alive.' "

New Mexico's Most Famous Book

What novel is thought to have had more American readers than any other book except the Bible? Why, *Ben-Hur,* of course. Although it is no longer on the best-seller list most people at least know the title, owing mainly to the celebrated film version which featured a spectacular chariot race.

By purest chance, the book is closely linked to New Mexico. Its author was Indiana native Lew Wallace—politician, diplomat and at one point the youngest Union general in the Civil War. In 1878 he won a presidential appointment as territorial governor of New Mexico. His task was to replace the current governor Samuel B. Axtell, a ruthless and unscrupulous despot who was a member of the notorious "Santa Fe Ring."

Wallace arrived in Santa Fe by buckboard late one September night. Rousing a justice of the territorial supreme court out of bed he had himself sworn in as governor. Then he sent a curt note to Axtell enclosing the president's order of removal. By the following morning Lew Wallace was firmly in control.

Over the next three years he became deeply involved in settling a little matter known as the Lincoln County War. At one stage he made an inspection tour of the battle zone and met with one of the war's leading combatants, Billy the Kid. Some time afterward the Kid is reputed to have announced: "I mean to ride up to the plaza at Santa Fe, hitch my horse in front of the palace, and put a bullet through Lew Wallace." If he actually said that it was idle boasting.

During his term Governor Wallace escaped the cares of his office through writing. In 1873 he had published a huge romantic novel called *The Fair God, A Tale of the Conquest of Mexico.* The book sold well in both America and England at two dollars a copy.

Even before coming to New Mexico, Wallace had outlined a new adventure novel set in the Near East during the early days of Christianity. To get the factual background straight he consulted hundreds of books on religion, history, geography, and botany in the Library of Congress. Lew Wallace believed in doing his homework.

At Santa Fe serious writing began on *Ben-Hur, A Tale of the Christ.*

Governor Lew Wallace. (Collection of the author.)

Wallace worked nights in the executive offices of the old Spanish governors' palace. Bent over a rough pine table, lighted by an oil lamp, he scratched out chapter after chapter.

Of that experience he said later: "The ghosts, if they were about, did not disturb me; yet in the hush of that gloomy room I beheld the Crucifixion, and strove to write what I beheld." Even today, his old study in the palace is pointed out to tourists as the "Ben-Hur Room."

On his business travels around the Territory the Governor always carried writing materials with him so that progress on the manuscripts would not be slowed. At Fort Stanton, on his trip to Lincoln in 1879,

Mrs. Wallace grew fearful that the lamp on his desk made him an illuminated target for Billy the Kid. Perhaps it was that fear and a general disenchantment with the Territory that led Mrs. Wallace later to write their son: "My Dear—We should have another war with Old Mexico to make her take back New Mexico."

Owing to the fame which *Ben Hur* afterward achieved an astonishing number of rooms around New Mexico soon were being pointed out as places where the Governor stopped in his travels and dashed off a chapter of his best-seller. Even today a dozen towns have old buildings containing a "Ben-Hur room," or so loyal residents will tell you. Had the Governor spent time in all these places writing the resulting book would have been of a size too heavy for the average reader to lift.

As it turned out, the volume was large enough. When published on November 12, 1880, the finished work contained 200,000 words. Against the backdrop of the life of Christ the fast-moving story of the hero Ben-Hur unfolds. A critic hailed it as "the finest historical novel of our time." But the public was slow to take to it.

For the first several years sales dragged. Then the book caught fire and by the end of a quarter-century *Ben-Hur* had solidly established itself as a classic. In 1884 Wallace wrote to his wife: "General U. S. Grant told me today that he read it through word for word; that he began in the morning, not having read a novel in ten years before, and finished it next day at noon, after reading all night."

Grant was not the only one becharmed. Cheap editions and luxurious editions flooded the market. *Ben-Hur* became a national fad and a favorite gift for all occasions.

In 1887 came the first of many dramatizations on the stage. When it was produced in New York in 1899, Lew Wallace arrived in town to watch the final rehearsals and to be present at the first performance. Advance publicity heralded it as the biggest play ever attempted, and the theater was mobbed.

At the premier author Wallace in his private box was the center of attention—at least until the chariot race. A treadmill had been installed on the stage, and two actual chariots, each pulled by four plunging Arabian horses, imparted a sense of reality not seen before on Broadway.

As the curtain fell, three hours and twenty-nine minutes after the start, the floor became pandemonium. There were curtain calls after curtain calls. Dignified Wallace stood to take his bows with the cast.

It was a fitting climax for a work that had been composed more than twenty years before and two thousand miles away in an ancient adobe palace on the Santa Fe plaza.

The Man Who Saved A President

In 1882 a frail, bearded man in his mid-fifties stepped off the Santa Fe train in Albuquerque. None of the other passengers paid much attention to him for in no way did he appear out of the ordinary. But that gentleman, thirteen years before, had cast a vote in the U.S. Congress which historians would one day call the most heroic act in American history.

Edmund G. Ross, an ex-senator from Kansas, had come to New Mexico to escape his past and begin a new life. For the rest of his days, he was to be closely associated with territorial politics.

Ross's troubles began in 1868. That year radical Republicans in Congress were attempting to impeach President Andrew Johnson because he had blocked their harsh moves to punish the South for the rebellion that led to the Civil War. On the day the bill of impeachment came up for a vote every senator's stand was already known—except one. Republican Edmund Ross of Kansas had announced that he would be strictly impartial and reach a decision on the evidence alone. Neither politics nor outside pressure would sway him.

Ross's vote was crucial for conviction since it was the last one the radicals needed to obtain the necessary two-thirds majority. As the roll was called and each senator announced his vote the chamber became deathly quiet. When the speaker reached the name of Edmund Ross spectators in the gallery held their breaths.

The senator from Kansas rose and resolutely uttered two words: "Not Guilty!" From every throat there came a gasp. The president had been saved. "At that moment," Ross later wrote, "I looked down into my own political grave."

The statement was no exaggeration. Newspapers in his home state denounced him as a Judas Iscariot. A thousand leading citizens sent him a telegram reading, "Kansas repudiates you as she does all perjurers and skunks." Foes in Washington attempted to smear his reputation, claiming that he had accepted a bribe for his vote. His life was threatened. The Republicans expelled him from the party.

Returning to Kansas Ross courageously tried to rebuild his career. He entered the Democratic party and ran again for the senate but suffered a sound defeat. In Kansas he was finished.

That he chose New Mexico as a place of exile was no accident. As one of the original founders of the AT&SF Railway he already knew much about the Territory. He had learned more from his brother-in-law, H. C. Bennett, who earlier had settled in Silver City, invested in nearby mines and was full of praise for the region.

Edmund Ross went to Albuquerque, however, not Silver City. There an old friend from Kansas, one of the few who remained loyal, was editor of a newspaper. The editor had offered him a job. The once mighty senator was grateful—even for a minor position on a small-town paper.

Before long Ross began dabbling in politics again, but as a Democrat. Local Republicans still considered him tainted and turned a cold shoulder.

Then in 1885 President Grover Cleveland, who had come to office on the Democratic ticket, appointed Edmund Ross to the Territorial governorship of New Mexico. Ross was known as an incorruptible reformer, and Cleveland hoped that he could straighten out politics in Santa Fe which had long been dominated by a shady Republican machine known as the "Santa Fe Ring."

Ross went to work with zeal. Honest and dedicated to reform, he did not mind stepping on toes. He hounded corrupt politicians. He championed women's rights long before that cause was popular. As a temperance advocate he refused to allow liquor to be served in the old adobe Governors' Palace on the plaza. He also tried to expose the fraud that surrounded the confirmation of ancient Spanish land grants.

Not unexpectedly he made powerful enemies. The Republicans hated him and worked hard to disrupt his administration. Cattlemen also joined the opposition. In southern New Mexico, particularly in Lincoln County, the hugh cattle ranchers were harassing small sheep raisers and trying to drive them out. Governor Ross, always a friend of the underdog, took the side of the sheepmen and attempted to provide them protection.

In 1889 Republican Benjamin Harrison became president and Ross was forced out of office. He moved to Deming and for three years published a small newspaper, the *Deming Headlight*. Then he returned to Albuquerque, his first home in New Mexico. During his declining years he lived on a small fruit farm in the valley and ran a job printing office—quite a come-down for a man who had once been at the center of political storms.

As he passed his eightieth birthday in 1906, Ross remained troubled that Kansas had never forgiven him. Then, just a couple of months before his death, the good word came, brought by an old associate, General Hugh Cameron. The general arrived in Albuquerque bearing a sheaf of letters from aging Republicans vindicating Ross's anti-impeachment vote and expressing regret for the mistreatment accorded him. Through hindsight, it was now clear that Ross's stand had preserved the independence of the presidency and rescued American democracy from a serious mistake.

Governor Edmund G. Ross. Photograph by Skelly's Art Studio. (Neg. no. 10753, courtesy Museum of New Mexico.)

Cameron had gotten the letters in a most unusual way. When Ross had left Kansas in disgrace, the general announced that he was withdrawing from society and would live in a tree on a bluff above the town of Lawrence until Kansas repented and admitted it had done the senator wrong. Except for occasional excursions for supplies, he stayed perched among the lofty boughs winter after winter, while his hair and beard grew waist-length. Such eccentricity caused General Cameron to become known as the "Kansas Hermit."

The turning of the century and waning of old political grudges prompted Ross's surviving enemies to rethink their earlier harsh actions towards him. By late 1906 Cameron was satisfied that he had enough documents. Descending from his tree, he made the long-delayed pilgrimage to Albuquerque.

Edmund G. Ross at last saw his name rubbed clean of stain. As if anticipating his own passing shortly afterward he is supposed to have exclaimed, "I will be a bigger man dead than I have been alive." That prediction was overly optimistic, for within a few decades his name was all but forgotten. Hardly anyone ever visited his grave in Albuquerque's Fairview Cemetery.

Then in 1956 John F. Kennedy published a book entitled *Profiles in Courage,* containing sketches of America's bravest political figures. One chapter recounted the life story of Senator Ross, belatedly bringing it to public view.

In this lies one of the small but bitter ironies of history. Edmund Ross saved the presidency of Andrew Johnson, who, as vice-president, had succeeded the assassinated Lincoln. John F. Kennedy, who helped restore Ross's reputation, was himself assassinated almost exactly a century after Lincoln and was succeeded by a vice-president named Johnson.

A Train Ride of Terror

Some years ago when the Santa Fe Railroad was preparing to cut back on its passenger service I caught one of the last trains running between Albuquerque and El Paso. It was a ride purely for pleasure since my sole purpose was to see from a chair car window the vast expanses of the Jornada del Muerto, that long stretch of desert extending for ninety miles down the center of New Mexico.

Except for a few ranches and the ribbon of steel rails the Jornada is practically deserted today. But in centuries past when the Camino Real echoed to the rumble of ox carts and the shout of teamsters it was witness to a considerable flow of traffic. When modern builders put in a new highway, they left the Jornada and laid down an asphalt road to the west beyond the Fray Cristobal and Caballo Mountains.

Going south from Albuquerque the Santa Fe tracks hug the east bank of the Rio Grande until at a point below Socorro they leave the valley and enter the arid Jornada. Several hours later trains emerge from the desert, rejoin the river at the railroad junction at Rincón, and thence continue on to Las Cruces and El Paso. When I made my trip the day was bright with sunshine and it was difficult to realize that early passengers on this same route had often gotten aboard at peril to their lives.

The danger came from the annual spring flood on the Rio Grande and from cloudbursts in the neighboring mountains that sent walls of water thundering down normally dry arroyos which fed into the main river channel. In flood time rails in the valley were often under a foot or more of chocolate-colored water, and bridges over the lateral arroyos were apt to be out. More than one train during the 1880s and 1890s plummeted to disaster of the end of a washed-out bridge.

Two children who rode the Santa Fe south when the Rio Grande was at flood stage in 1884 recalled in later years the terror of that journey. They were Maude and Ralph McFie traveling from Illinois with their twenty-four-year-old mother. Some months before their father had preceded them to take a new job at the U.S. Land Office in Las Cruces and purchase a home for his family.

Trouble began soon after the train departed Albuquerque. As the McFies peered nervously through the car windows it seemed as if the engine were dragging them through a vast swirling lake. Time after time, they came to a complete halt at little marooned towns where they waited hours on end for the tracks to clear.

93

Work train with locomotive 85 (Baldwin, 1879) at Engle, New Mexico, ca. 1900. Photograph by E. J. Westervelt. (Neg. no. 35876, courtesy Museum of New Mexico.)

Because of the delays, drinking water soon gave out and many of the passengers went to the door where they dipped up brown river water in their cups. Mrs. McFie was afraid to let her children partake of the dirty stuff, but luckily a bag of oranges she carried helped quench their thirst.

At last they reached the Jornada and escaped the flood. The interval in the desert allowed the weary travelers to grab some much needed sleep, although the lack of water was proving a real hardship. Then they entered the valley once more and the ordeal was renewed.

Mrs. McFie tried to calm the children by telling them that at Rincón Junction, where a change of trains was to be made, they would surely find a good eating house and plenty of clear, pure water. But when they arrived there was no time either for dinner or a drink. The shuttle train from El Paso, consisting of an engine and a single yellow chair car, had just come in from the south, and the engineer said they must start back at once if they were to have any chance of getting through. The flood was rising fast.

The main train from Albuquerque was continuing on west to California, which meant that at Rincón it had to cross a huge arroyo. Water was up to the ties on the steel railroad bridge, and bystanders at the station and passengers on the shuttle watched and held their breaths while the long string of cars braved the wide, wide river. The west-bound made it to the far bank—but just barely.

For the McFie family the last forty miles to their destination at Las Cruces proved the worst. They were not reassured when someone told them that the companion train to this one had been swept away just the year before as it was coming down the Mesilla Valley.

Little Maude and Ralph left their plush red seats and went to the end of the coach to ask the conductor for some water. They had not had a sip all day. The poor man looked startled. The train had left Rincón so fast no drinking water had been taken on. "Not a word to your mother about this," he warned. "She's upset enough as it is."

As the children went back to their seats they literally waded, for the river was inside the car. Mrs. McFie had her palms pressed to the window glass and was staring into the inky darkness. Night had overtaken them. Suddenly perceiving that the floodwaters were just a few inches below the sill and that waves were lapping all around, she became hysterical.

Jumping from her seat, she ran splashing up and down the aisle. "We must stop the train and back up to Rincón. Or we'll all be lost," the poor woman cried. The conductor and a brakeman gently subdued her and carried her back to her place.

One of them found a bottle of Kentucky whiskey someplace and poured a generous cupful. "Down this, ma'am, and you'll feel a lot better." Crying and gagging, Mrs. McFie gulped the amber liquid. She was a good Presbyterian and not accustomed to spirits. Before long the "medicine" did its work and she was blessedly drunk and then asleep.

The plucky youngsters pulled their feet up on the seats to keep them dry, and wide-eyed through the long night they let out not a whisper. With the first light of dawn they reached Las Cruces and there was their father waiting anxiously on the platform. The terrible train ride was over.

After unloading the McFies the shuttle headed on for El Paso. Just a few miles down the line, it went off a washed-out trestle and toppled into the raging torrent.

Weeks later, when the flood had receded, throngs of curious drove their buggies out from Las Cruces to see the engine and yellow coach lying on their sides. The Santa Fe Railroad had not even bothered to salvage them. Seeing the engine bell half-buried in the mud, Mrs. McFie announced, "We must have that bell for the new church we are building." Under her prodding the local Presbyterian congregation raised a fund and purchased the bell from the Railroad. Soon it was raised in the tower, becoming the first Protestant church bell in the Mesilla Valley.

Every Sunday morning when it was rung, Mrs. McFie was reminded of her harrowing introduction to "this God-forsaken New Mexico," as she always referred to the land that had become her new home.

The Shooting Spree of the High Fives

It has often been said that the American frontier came to an end in 1890. At least by that date there were no large blocks of unsettled country left for pioneering. But if the frontier was gone, some of the violence of the Old West still lingered. That was clearly demonstrated by the far-flung activities of an outlaw gang that terrorized southern New Mexico and southeastern Arizona during most of 1897. Head of the unruly band was William T. Christian, alias "Black Jack."

Christian, it would seem, was born to a life of crime. Though north Texas was his birthplace, both he and his older brother Robert spent their later youth in the lawless Oklahoma Territory. The pair engaged in petty robberies until the day a deputy sheriff cornered and tried to arrest them. Robert shot the deputy dead.

Convicted of the killing, the Christian brothers were hustled off to a lock-up in Oklahoma City. But when friends slipped guns into their cell they shot their way to freedom, killing the chief of police in the bargain. After a series of train and store robberies they vanished from Oklahoma.

Unfortunately, the outlaws picked New Mexico as their new field of operations. They first showed up in the Seven Rivers country along the Pecos River south of Artesia. There they remained only a couple of months.

Moving west, they went to cowboying just across the Arizona line in Cochise County. Soon the Christians made contact with three other young men who were wanted by the law. One was George Musgrave, a fugitive from a cattle rustling charge at Roswell. The other two, Code Young and Bob Hayes, also had a history of stealing stock. They, together with Will and Robert Christian, formed a gang known as the High Fives after a popular card game of the day.

The outlaws' first target was the store and post office at Separ, New Mexico, a whistle stop between Lordsburg and Deming. They executed the job without any trouble but got away with only $250 in cash and goods. That set the pattern for the gang's career. Through dozens of subsequent hold-ups they seldom got more than that amount. The High Fives seemed jinxed.

Acknowledged leader of the band was the younger Christian, William. Tipping the scales at over two hundred pounds, he had been dubbed "Black Jack" by cowboy acquaintances because of his dark complexion. The High Fives were often referred to in the territorial press as Black Jack's Gang.

On August 6, 1897, they tried to stick up the bank in Nogales, Arizona, but the whole affair was badly bungled. In a shoot-out the boys barely escaped with their lives. Since the country swarmed with posses they headed back for New Mexico.

Next the High Fives tried a nighttime robbery of the A & P train southwest of Albuquerque. They got the engine stopped and were preparing to blow open the express car with twelve sticks of dynamite. Code Young walked back toward the passenger cars when suddenly a deputy U.S. Marshall who happened to be aboard popped out and killed him with a load of buckshot.

The rest of the gang was so unnerved that all jumped on their horses and rode away empty-handed. Regrouping a few days later they began plundering stagecoaches running between Socorro and White Oaks, down in Lincoln County. In this interval George Musgrave briefly left his outlaw companions and rode over to Roswell. There he mercilessly gunned down a cowboy against whom he held an old grudge.

Since pickings were slim and the country getting hotter Black Jack and the three remaining gang members headed back for their old haunts in Arizona. On the way they raided Separ again, getting even less this time—a mere hundred dollars. A string of new robberies carried out in Cochise and neighboring counties brought out lawmen in force. Among them were U.S. marshalls, county sheriffs, Wells Fargo & Co. special officers, railroad agents and post office inspectors.

The desperados went into hiding at a remote cabin in the Las Animas Mountains of southwestern New Mexico, but a posse tracked them down. In a blaze of gunfire Bob Hayes fell mortally wounded. But the two Christians and Musgrave fought their way out and escaped.

After finding several new recruits Black Jack established another hideout just across the Arizona border. Several hold-ups that he engineered fell flat, which should have suggested to him by now that he was in the wrong business.

On April 28 the gang was ambushed again and one of the members, shot in the hip, died a few hours later from the wound. Several of the posse identified the deceased as Black Jack Christian, though none had ever seen him up close.

The two surviving High Fivers, Robert Christian and George Musgrave, finally pulled a profitable robbery the following November. They successfully held up the eastbound train at Grants and got away with cash rumored to be in six figures. It is known that they escaped into Chihuahua where Robert vanishes from history. Musgrave, so records tell us, fled to South America where he died in 1947.

Another famous outlaw, Black Jack Ketchum, has often been confused with Black Jack Christian. Ketchum, a notorious train robber in the Clayton area, claimed he had never been a part of the other Black Jack's gang.

He also stated this: "The man they killed in Arizona was not Black Jack Christian. He is not dead to my certain knowledge. Oh, yes; I have an idea where he is, but I won't tell."

These words were uttered on the morning of April 26, 1901, a few hours before Ketchum was led to the gallows and hung for his crimes.

A Bar Cross Christmas

The cowboy had a strong attachment to Christmas. Living a hard and dangerous life, often far removed from his family, he looked upon that December holiday as the year's high point. The lore of the Southwest is filled with tales about sentimental range riders who undertook some special act of Christmas charity.

One of my favorites was related many years ago by Eugene Rhodes, among New Mexico's most celebrated western writers. The story was based on a true incident that occurred before the turn of the century on the Bar Cross Ranch.

The Bar Cross then took in several hundred square miles of desert and mountains west of the Tularosa Basin. It employed more than two score cowboys. Among them the low man on the totem pole was the horse wrangler, who in this case happened to be an under-sized teenager named John Graham.

Nothing was known about him, except that he could ride a bronc as well as any of the crew and that he was a steady and loyal hand. But there was another matter that caused serious damage to his reputation.

In appearance John Graham looked like a hobo. His clothes were ragged, his bedroll was shabby, and he rode a cheap, worn saddle bought long ago with Arbuckle coffee coupons. He had no gloves at all.

"Stingy and a miser," was what his fellow cowboys called him behind his back and to his face. Why didn't he spend some of his $25-a-month wages on new gear? He was giving the Bar Cross brand a bad name.

"Way I figure it," said cowboy Hiram Yost at the campfire one evening, "John is saving every penny so he can buy this ranch one day and we'll all be working for him."

"Them duds he wears and that old Arbuckle is a disgrace to the outfit," chimed in another hand. "Why don't you fire him?" he asked the foreman.

And the foreman replied, "I suppose I would fire him in a minute, except he's a first rate rider and roper."

This conversation, similar to many earlier ones, took place at the end of the round-up in late November. The crew—all except John out bedding down the horseherd—was relaxing at the fire after a heavy meal.

With them that evening was a Mr. Cole, the cattle buyer who came to the ranch yearly at this time to look over the stock and make a purchase.

He listened attentively to the complaints against young Graham, the same ones he had heard after the previous round-up.

"That John," someone was saying to him now, "has a new name in these parts. We call him the Bar Cross Liar. That's 'cause when we asked him if he was coming to the big Christmas Eve dance in Engle, he said he couldn't. Allowed as how he was broke and unable to buy good clothes. What a lie! He's probably got more money saved up than any five of us."

"He is a liar all right," Mr. Cole said softly, "but not quite in the way you mean. I was waiting for the train over at Magdalena last week and got to talking with a fellow working in his little garden next to the station. He had a shack house, a wife, two small daughters and he said his name was Graham.

"For several months he'd been sick," Cole continued, "and couldn't work at freighting. Finally he had to sell his team and freight wagon to pay the doctor and store bills. Just now getting back on his feet but couldn't find a job. Only thing keeping the family afloat was a son working down on the Bar Cross Ranch who was sending part of his wages home."

And Mr. Cole concluded: "The man pulled out a crumpled letter from his pocket and gave it to me to read. It was from his son. About then his wife called him into the shack for something and while he was gone I made a quick copy of that letter. Have it right here," he announced as he passed the paper to Hiram Yost.

Hiram read quickly, turned a deep red under his leathery tan and handed the letter to the man next to him. When it had gone around the circle the Bar Cross crew remained tight-lipped and silent for several minutes. They were not used to experiencing shame, but they felt it now.

Hiram Yost finally spoke: "Seems we got some fence-mending to do before Christmas. There'll be a collection to take up first. The boys at the 7TX will want in on this and the EC outfit, too. We'll need a top rate saddle and a Navajo blanket."

"A new suit of clothes," volunteered a voice from the circle.

"A good Stetson," from another.

"Boots, of course."

"Decent spurs."

And so it went, until the foreman said soberly, "Gear is fine, but it's the Graham family that needs help. The ranch could use a man at Aleman to tend the windmill and give our boys supplies when they ride through. And there's a good house there. I can help, too, by boosting John's wages to thirty dollars a month."

During the next few weeks the Bar Cross punchers were full of business. One of their number was sent to El Paso for a new saddle and clothes. The Grahams came down from Magdalena and were installed at Aleman. They were astonished to find a full pantry and plenty of household furnishings, which the cowboys sheepishly said had been left by the last tenant and they were welcome to.

Horse round-up on the Maxwell Land Grant in New Mexico, ca. 1893.

(Neg. no. 15137, courtesy Museum of New Mexico.)

When Mrs. Graham asked about her son, absent from home almost two years, she was told that he had been assigned to a distant horse camp and could not be spared. But he would be down to Engle on Christmas Eve for the feasting and dancing and they would see him there.

On the twenty-fourth Hiram Yost rode to the horse camp where John, since close of the round-up, had been living alone tending the herd and gentling broncs.

"You're wanted. That's orders," he told the lad gruffly.

"Should I take my bed roll?" John asked, thoroughly confused.

"Might as well," Hiram replied, "you won't need it here any more."

John Graham was thunderstruck. Those words could mean only one thing. He was being fired! Some of the boys, he knew, had been urging the foreman to do just that. Now it had happened.

As the pair rode toward Engle in the gathering gloom Hiram noted that his companion, clad only in a thin coat, clenched his teeth against the cold and the fate that awaited him.

Meanwhile, at Engle people from fifty miles around were arriving for the festivities. Long tables had been set up in the freshly swept dance hall and tempting holiday food heaped upon them. The Graham family arrived and were given seats up front. Their son would come in later, they were told. And when they asked why a shiny saddle sat on a keg in the center of the room, surrounded by an array of cowboy gear and garb, no one gave them an answer.

As the crowd sat down to eat the Bar Cross foreman rapped for attention. "I have a few words to say about one of our men, John Graham. But first, I want to read a letter that fell into my hands."

He unfolded the paper given him by Mr. Cole and read:
"Dear Mother and Father:

I'm feeling fine. It's cold nights, but one of the hands bought an overcoat and gave me his old one, almost good as new. The boys are awful fine to me. And I bought myself a new pair of gloves. The boss raised me to $35 so I can keep sending you the $25 as usual 'cause I don't need it. I got a new suit of clothes for Christmas Eve and I'll have a good time at the dance . . ."

"There's more to this letter," spoke the foreman painfully, "but I needn't go on. It's just nothing but lies. John said he had plenty of new clothes. He didn't. He said we treated him nice, when, in fact, we treated him like dirt and called him stingy. And he said he was coming to this Christmas dance when he really meant to stay alone in that Godforsaken horse camp."

Before he could go farther there came the sound of two horses approaching outside. The Grahams were hastily shunted into a side room and the door shut. The room fell perfectly quiet.

John dismounted, took one look at the brightly lit dance hall and told Hiram that he would slip in the back door to get warm.

"No such thing young fellow, you're going in the front," Yost announced sternly, taking his arm.

Suddenly John Graham was propelled through the door and across the floor toward the finest mountain of Christmas gifts ever assembled in that part of the Territory. As his jaw dropped someone yelled, "The guest of honor has arrived!" And cheers shook the rafters of the Engle dance hall.

"This is your night, John," boomed the foreman.

Before the young man could reply he was shoved again—this time into a small side room and the waiting arms of his family. The last words he heard before the door closed were from Hiram Yost, who proclaimed loudly: "There goes our Bar Cross Liar. The truest and best man on the ranch!"

Pablo Abeita, Governor of Isleta Pueblo. Photograph by J. R. Willis. (Neg. no. 42286, courtesy Museum of New Mexico.)

Pablo and the President

Until his death in 1940 Pablo Abeita was the most colorful and prominent resident of Isleta Indian pueblo, located a dozen miles south of Albuquerque. Isleta is the southernmost New Mexico pueblo and also the parent of the village of Ysleta del Sur below El Paso, which was founded by Indian refugees after the revolt of 1680.

Pablo Abeita operated a store in his village for many years. But it was his entry into politics rather than his merchandising ability that spread his fame beyond the limits of Isleta. He became one of the leading spokesmen for Indian rights both in New Mexico and Washington. In public statements and frequent letters to the press he denounced misguided policies of the Indian Bureau and criticized in general many silly Anglo notions.

In addition to speaking his native language he was fluent and literate in both Spanish and English. He was an avid reader and considered one of the best educated Indians in the state. St. Michael's College (now the College of Santa Fe) awarded him the honorary degrees of Master of Ancient History and Doctor of Philosophy.

On numerous occasions Pablo Abeita journeyed to the nation's capital to represent the interests of his people at the White House and before Congress. By his own claim he was the only Indian who personally met all the presidents of the United States, from Grover Cleveland in 1886 to FDR in 1936.

Dr. Abeita had a wry sense of humor. Even when criticizing his political foes he made his points with quaint sarcasm rather than malicious barbs. And he loved a joke, especially if he could put one over on the Anglos.

One of his favorite stories involved a series of encounters with President Teddy Roosevelt. It began when Abeita accompanied a large Indian delegation to Washington soon after TR had come to office in 1901. The group was ushered into the President's chamber and received with cordial handshakes and a brief but kindly speech. As they were leaving, an official aid came up to Pablo Abeita, tugged at his sleeve and whispered for him to stay behind as the President wanted to see him alone.

When the others had gone Roosevelt said, "Pablo, sit down. I want to know all about your village and what the Indians need."

Abeita launched into a lengthy speech, but he hurried as fast as possible knowing that the President was a busy man. After a time several cabinet members wandered in and sat impatiently by waiting to get a word in. One of them in exasperation finally took out his watch and pointed at it. Perturbed, President Roosevelt turned around and said, "Gentlemen, I'm fully aware of the time we are spending here. Go on, Pablo." The orator from Isleta continued for two hours and twenty minutes.

As he was departing he was told by the President, "Pablo, some day I'm coming to Isleta and I want to visit you in your home."

Later there would be those who would express doubt that this incident really happened. After all, they asked, why should TR have singled out Pablo Abeita and shown such interest in one small New Mexico pueblo? The answer is an easy one though.

Teddy Roosevelt's principal adviser on Indian affairs was the celebrated western writer Charles Lummis. In the early 1890s Lummis had lived at Isleta collecting folk tales. As he was well acquainted with the village and its people it is safe to assume that he had filled the President's ear before the interview with Abeita.

A few months later Pablo Abeita was working in his store when he received a message. It said that Roosevelt was in Albuquerque staying at the Alvarado Hotel and wanted to see him. Hitching his team to a farm wagon, he drove up and tied the horses in front of the hotel.

Inside he ran square into two federal agents standing guard. They wanted to know his business. And his name.

"I haven't got any name," Pablo Abeita replied. He was having one of his little jokes, knowing that these green easterners would believe anything about Indians—even that they went nameless. "Tell the President an Indian wants to see him," he added.

A hot argument got started. As the noise increased Roosevelt heard the commotion and came out of his suite. When he saw Pablo Abeita in the middle of a crowd that had gathered he elbowed through, grabbed him by the arm and dragged him through the door.

"Pablo, you didn't think I'd really come, did you?" chuckled the President. "Now how will we get out to Isleta without all that crowd following us?"

The situation posed no problem for Indian ingenuity. Pablo Abeita took his host's hat and coat, placed them under the bright blanket he always wore, and carried the garments outside where he stowed them safely in his wagon. Then picking up another blanket he returned to the hotel.

Next he wrapped the President, native fashion, in the spare blanket so that his face and head were covered. Then shuffling along in proper style the pair passed through the lobby and safely gained the street.

Whipping his horses to a gallop, Abeita carried the President of the United States to his home and fed him lunch. Afterward he delivered him back at the Alvarado.

Walking again into the lobby they found the place overflowing with people. Secret Service men were dashing everywhere in great excitement because they had lost the President.

Pablo Abeita did not overlook the comic aspect of the scene and he saw a chance to add to it. In the middle of the floor, he let out a thunderous war whoop. Once he had gained universal attention he jerked the blanket off Roosevelt's head as if he were unveiling a surprise package. People stared and their jaws dropped.

Agents came running from all sides, much put out because the President had gotten away from them.

As Abeita recounted it in later years to journalist Ernie Pyle, TR appeared wholly unconcerned. "Boys," he said, "I was just as safe in Pablo's hands as I am with anybody in the world."

First Airplanes on the Rio Grande

The history of aviation in New Mexico apparently had its beginnings at the Territorial Fair in Albuquerque. In 1910 fair secretary Roy Stamm imported a primitive airplane on a railroad flatcar. Advance posters promised the contraption's first flight would be the most sensational attraction ever witnessed in the West.

Fair visitors crowded around to view the strange craft as it sat on the ground. But they never saw it fly. At Albuquerque's high altitude the plane's engine power was insufficient for a take-off.

Undaunted, Stamm contracted the next year with famous stunt pilot Charles F. Walsh to make three flights of fifteen minutes each in his single propeller Curtis biplane. The craft was shipped in by railway express, assembled at the fairgrounds and made its scheduled flights over the city.

On his first excursion Walsh circled over the Fair baseball diamond while a game was in progress, dropping small sacks of flour on the players. Intended as a prank, the Albuquerque press took note of the more ominous implicatons: "It demonstrated clearly the practicability of the use of the biplane as an implement of war, since it would be possible to drop bombs on an army or battleship with deadly effect."

On the final run Walsh agreed to take aloft Roy Stamm's younger brother Raymond. A short board was wired to the lower wing to serve as a seat, and an anvil was tied to the end of the biplane as a weight equalizer. Unscientific perhaps, the additions proved quite functional. With Raymond Stamm seated on the board, his feet hanging free and his arms clutching a wing strut, Walsh soared on a three-mile circuit from the fairgrounds. The brief trip set a world's record—the first time a passenger had been lifted and carried from five thousand feet above sea level.

The aerial show was rated a resounding success. An attempt was made in 1912 to get Walsh back for a repeat performance. However, he had already accepted an engagement at the New Jersey State Fair. So he sent as a replacement his former teacher and the man who had led him to stunt flying, the renowned barnstormer Lincoln Beachey.

The day after Beachey's arrival in Albuquerque word was received

Take-off at the Territorial Fair, Albuquerque. (Collection of the author.)

of Walsh's death. Before a crowd of 65,000 at Trenton, he had been making a spiral manuever when the biplane went out of control and crashed from an altitude of 2,000 feet. Said the grisly news reports, "Practically every bone in the aviator's body was broken."

Shortly afterward Walsh's remains, accompanied by his young widow, passed through Albuquerque en route to burial at his home in San Diego. Lincoln Beachey and Raymond Stamm were at the depot, flowers in hand, when the Limited made a brief stop. Mrs. Walsh cried on the elder man's shoulder when they met.

"Lincoln, if it wasn't for you, Charlie would be alive today," she wept. She had never approved of air acrobatics.

The moment was solemn for Raymond Stamm as well. By coincidence the encounter with Mrs. Walsh occurred one year to the day after his world record flight with her husband.

Filled with remorse, Lincoln Beachey swore he would never fly again. But the pull of the skies was too strong. Two years later, while stunt flying at the San Francisco Exposition, a wing fell off his plane and he dropped into the bay and was lost.

One other landmark in New Mexico's aeronautical history can be noted. In 1913, Roy N. Francis of California brought a twin propeller tractor biplane to the fair. It had far more power than the Curtis plane used by Walsh and was capable of carrying three or four passengers. Roy Stamm went on one of the flights with a high-speed camera and took the first aerial photographs of Albuquerque, probably the first ever made anywhere in the Southwest.

Books of Related Interest
from Ancient City Press

THE ADOBE BOOK, by John F. O'Connor. 1973.
Detailed how-to covering every phase of construction.

COLONIAL FRONTIERS: Art and Life in Spanish New Mexico,
The Fred Harvey Collection, edited by Christine Mather. 1983.
Exhibition catalogue with major papers on colonial Mexico and New
Mexico by Mather, Marc Simmons, Richard Ahlborn and Bertha Dutton.
A publication of the Museum of International Folk Art sponsored by
the International Folk Art Foundation.

ECHOES OF THE FLUTE, by Lorenzo de Córdova. 1972 (2d printing 1982).
Old Hispanic village Lenten, funeral and Penitente Brotherhood cus-
toms in northern New Mexico.

THE GENUINE NEW MEXICO TASTY RECIPES,
by Cleofas M. Jaramillo. 1981.
Reprint of rare 1942 cookbook with seventy-five delicious old-time New
Mexican Spanish recipes and additional materials on traditional Hispano
food.

HISPANIC ARTS AND ETHNOHISTORY IN THE SOUTHWEST:
New Papers Inspired by the Work of E. Boyd,
edited by Marta Weigle with Claudia Larcombe
and Samuel Larcombe. 1983.
Twenty-two articles by twenty-three scholars, including Marc Simmons,
on traditional Hispanic arts, their preservation, and 17-19th-century life
in New Mexico. A Spanish Colonial Arts Society book published by
Ancient City Press and the University of New Mexico Press.

NEW MEXICO ARTISTS AND WRITERS: A Celebration, 1940,
edited and compiled by Marta Weigle and Kyle Fiore. 1982.
Oversized newspaper with facsimile reprint of June 26, 1940, special
38-page edition of *The Santa Fe New Mexican,* "Prominent Artists and
Writers of New Mexico," with additional contemporaneous materials.

THE PENITENTES OF THE SOUTHWEST, by Marta Weigle.
1970 (3d printing 1982).
> History and description of Brotherhood organization, rites and arts.

SANTA FE AND TAOS: The Writer's Era, 1916-1941,
by Marta Weigle and Kyle Fiore. 1982.
> Writers', publishers' and printers' civic and literary activities chronicled and illustrated; articles by D. H. Lawrence, Mabel Dodge Luhan, Ruth Laughlin and Elizabeth Shepley Sergeant.

SANTOS AND SAINTS: The Religious Folk Art of Hispanic New Mexico,
by Thomas J. Steele, S. J. Reprint of 1974 ed. with 1982 update.
> Historical, sociological and theological analysis of Hispanic folk art and religion in New Mexico.

EL SANTUARIO DE CHIMAYO, by Stephen F. de Borhegyi and E. Boyd. 1956 (1982 printing).
> History and detailed description of the famous healing shrine north of Santa Fe. A Spanish Colonial Arts Society book.

SHADOWS OF THE PAST, by Cleofas M. Jaramillo. 1980 reprint of the 1941 Seton Village Press ed.
> Family history and firsthand account of Hispanic folklore and customs in 19th-century northern New Mexico.

The companion to *Ranchers, Ramblers and Renegades: True Tales of Territorial New Mexico,* by Marc Simmons, is now available through Ancient City Press:

TAOS TO TOMÉ: True Tales of Hispanic New Mexico, by Marc Simmons. 1978.
> Twenty-one vignettes of life and lives in pioneer New Mexico, 1540-1850.